The

Consciousness of Righteousness

How to Release God's Power within You!

Joseph Edhuine

I

THE CONSCIOUSNESS OF RIGHTEOUSNESS
How to Release God's Power within You!

ISBN-13: 978-1978484344
ISBN-10: 1978484348

DEDICATION

I dedicate this book to those who believe in the lies of
the devil that they are sinners saved by grace and
that they have to work hard here on
Earth to be righteous in Heaven.

I also devote this book to those who chose to believe in
the revelation of the Word of God instead of the
word of the devil.

For those who feel dirty, those who feel they have
no personal value and those who feel that God
never answers their prayers;
I wrote this book with you in mind.

Finally, I dedicate this book to my lovely wife Cynthia
Lynne, whom I love dearly, who encourages me and
believes in the abilities God reveals today, and also to
my children whom I love deeply.

TABLE OF CONTENTS

Righteousness Lost

Righteousness Promised

Righteousness Preached

Righteousness Restored

Living the Consciousness of Righteousness

Obstacles to a Consciousness of Righteousness

An Overview of A.W.A.R.E.

INTRODUCTION

At some point in your life, you think to yourself, "It is just not happening for me". At some point, you begin to think that things are not working out for you. At some point, you begin to doubt; you begin to fear. You keep praying and praying, but it just seems like you cannot get a break. It seems that God is just not answering your prayers.

I say you *think* these things because you dare not say them. You dare not state them aloud. Oh no, not out loud. But you do *think* them. Then you realize that just by thinking those negative thoughts, that you have just done the worst thing in the world that you could possibly do...you began to doubt!

Oh my God! Doubt is the killer. Once you doubt, you guarantee that God never answers your prayers. Once doubt creeps in, you know you will never see the manifestation of your prayers.

When you begin to doubt, it is certain that you will not get that job.

Once you start to doubt, there is no way you will ever get that house. You expressed doubt and now you are never going to get out of debt. You cannot doubt.

You must have faith. You must have faith and you know that.

However, when you think about it, you realize that you *have* had faith for the last three years. You have maintained the faith for the last 10 years, 15 years or 32 years. You have faithfully kept on and continued to praise God for the longest time. You continued to believe that which you could not see. You continued to believe that God would supply all your needs in abundance; even though this is the fourth time you have received an eviction notice.

You continue to believe God will bless you with a job even though you have been unemployed for nearly eight months as you keep looking and searching.

You continue to believe what it says in the Bible, that, *"All things will work for the good for those who love the Lord,"* and God knows that you love Him with all your heart and soul. You continue to believe even though you also continue to struggle and fight just to keep your head above water.

The bills are piled up, almost all of your mail comes in pink and red envelopes; if you don't make that utility payment by tomorrow the lights will be shut off and, oh my God, you forgot to pay your tithes!

But you continue to shout, "Hallelujah!" for other people as you stand by and watch as God showers them with blessings and favor. You are happy for her that God blessed her with a new car. You were happy for him when the Lord miraculously provided him with that new job. You are genuinely happy for them, even though you know that they are not half as dedicated to the Lord as you are.

You listen to the testimony and hear how God blessed that family beyond all expectation and imagination and you shout, "Amen, won't He do it?"

Yes, He will. And deep down inside you silently think, "…Maybe He just won't do it for me."

Deep down inside you, way down in your gut, something says to you, "Look at that. *He* gets a great job like that and he doesn't even serve on any ministries and doesn't do anything in the church."

Way down, deep in your soul, you think, "God blessed her with a wonderful husband like that and here I have been looking and praying for 12 years…"

Then it hits you like a ton of bricks! Stop! It's the devil! The devil is a liar! You are too mature in Christ to be feeling like that. You know it is the devil putting those horrible thoughts in your head. So, you stop and start praising His name for real, "Jesus, Jesus."

However, still lingering back in your mind is a still small voice that says, "But when is it ever going to happen for me? When am I ever going to get my blessing?"

Oh my God! There you go again! You are doing it again! Lord have mercy! Stop! You have to repent and start all over, "Lord, I repent from those doubtful thoughts; I repent from speaking death…"

Have you ever felt this way? Have you ever been in the whirlpool cycle of faith, fear, doubt, disbelief, repentance and back to faith? Let me tell you, I know how you feel. Do you hear what I say?

I know how you feel because I have been there. I tell you the truth; I have been in that seemingly blasphemous chain of thought that sometimes seems almost impossible to get out of your mind. However, God revealed the answer to me; a truth that you have actually known all along, and I will reveal it to you shortly.

But at first, you are totally faithful. No matter what happened, no matter what you saw, no matter what the world threw at you; you remained faithful and strong. You were in church and raising your

4

hands and praising God as if you had already received the blessings you had been seeking.

Then, some time goes by and you don't see any results. You keep the faith.

More time, no results.

You pray and read the Word and claim the victory in the name of Jesus!

More time, few results.

You start praying more, fasting and praying. More time goes by, but you *know* that sometimes it takes time, Amen?

Then you look up and it's been years.

You Must Have Faith

When the negative thoughts of doubt begin to overwhelm you, you know the answer. The answer is that you must have faith. You must maintain the faith. Praise God! You have to stay steadfast, immoveable, grounded and rooted in the faith. Amen?

Come on now. You are no spring chicken. You know the Word. Keep the faith no matter what things look like at any particular moment.

But then you realize that you are *not* a spring chicken or a babe in Christ. You realize that you have been in the Word for many years. You know that you do not know everything but you know that you have grown. You have matured a little over the years.

You look up and you realize that you have kept the faith for years. You have maintained the faith in the face of the worst realities for five years now. Maybe you have kept your faith going without doubt for ten years, or eighteen years or thirty-seven years. My God, come to think about it, it has been a long time.

It has been so long. So long that you have been keeping the faith, studying the Word, staying in prayer; but when you think about it, things have still not really seemed to work out for you.

How long have you been praying that the Lord bless you with a husband? How long has it been? You know that you needed just to believe, and you know that He will do anything that we ask. But how long has it been?

You have been praying for a new job, praying to get out of debt, praying for a child. You fervently prayed for a house. You prayed for the pain to go away. You prayed for relief to the diabetes and the high blood pressure. You have been praying and praying and praying.

Then one day you figure it out. Maybe it was a sermon, or something you read; you are not exactly sure when or where you heard it, but now it finally makes sense to you.

Yes, all of that praying is one thing, but you have not been praying the right way! You realize that you have been praying and asking God to do things *for* you. No, no, no! That's not it.

God gave *us* the power. God gave *you* the power. You need to pray and *command* things to happen. Amen!

That's it. That's it! You have heard this before a thousand times, but suddenly it all makes sense. You have not been commanding things to happen. You have been asking and waiting. But the Word says that you need to *command*, you need to direct, you need to tell.

You've been asking the mountain to please move out of the way. No! You have to *tell* the mountain to get up and be cast into the sea! Tell it! Command it!

So, you change it up. You change your approach to prayer in every way. Now you command in the name of Jesus! Now you've got the power. Now things will begin to happen.

A few weeks, a few months go by and you sadly realize that still, not much has changed. At first when you started to command things, it looked as though there was some light at the end of the tunnel. You believed so strongly. You were in complete faith. Then it seemed for every step forward you made, there came two steps back.

You commanded that you would be financially free, and things started to happen. You got spending under control, got a raise on your job and you finally made the last payment on the car! Hallelujah! That's one huge weight lifted. You are on your way!

Then, the car broke down. You never had any problems out of the car since the day you bought it, but now the repair bill comes out to total more money than three months of car payments. There goes the little emergency fund that you were just starting to build up. It knocks the preverbal wind out of you.

Is this you? Have you ever felt this way? Be honest. We all go through momentary bouts of doubt. The only thing is that for many of us, in fact, for most of us, it is not momentary; it is continuous. It is a long continuous thought process.

Then you start to become settled in. You continue to go to church, read and study the Word and praise God, week after week month after month for years. All the while harboring that thought in the back of your mind, "When is it going to happen for me?"

You seem to settle down and accept your position and lot in life. Now, in your Christian maturity, you know that you have to be patient, after all, everything happens in God's time. You know the old saying, *"He may not come when you want Him, but He is always right on time"*.

So you settle into waiting patiently. You still struggle to keep your head above water. You still struggle with disease, sickness and health issues. You still struggle with addiction. You are still alone and without a mate. You are still barren and without children. You still battle sin every day.

You have kept the faith and put work behind it; but nothing has changed. The Lord has still not yet answered your prayers. What is wrong? What is the problem?

Then, finally, a revelation hits you. Thank you Holy Ghost! You receive a life changing revelation. Now you know what has been missing! You know exactly what the problem has been. After all these years, you finally have the answer!

The answer is that you have never received the infilling of the Holy Spirit! Praise be to God; that's it!

You know what the Word says. You know what the Bible says in Acts 1:8 that,

"...you will receive power when the Holy Spirit comes on you;..."

My God, that is it and has been the problem for all of these years! Jesus, The Christ Himself, did not even begin His ministry on Earth until He was first baptized by water and then by the Holy Spirit. That's it.

How could you have missed this essential teaching all of these years? Maybe your church and pastor does not teach the baptism of the Holy Spirit. Many churches do not even talk about such doctrine. But it is there, in the Word of God. Do you hear what I say?

All you need do is get the baptism of the Holy Spirit and finally, once and for all, everything will turn around.

So, you get the baptism of the Holy Spirit and you show evidence by speaking in tongues; glory to God! Now, oh yes, now, things will finally begin to happen for you, and, lo and behold they do! That is, at first anyway.

Right away, it appears that you see some change. You begin to see a few things happen for you. You certainly have a better and clearer understanding of scripture and you have the gift of discernment.

Speaking of gifts, you find that God has blessed you with the gift of healing. It doesn't seem to work every time, which has to be due to the lack of faith in the one being healed. However, you have laid hands on people and seen them healed, glory to God!

Strange though, it looks like even though you have healed others, you can't seem to heal yourself! How can this be? You have the power of God in your hands and in your touch, yet you cannot make that pain in your back go away. You healed a woman who was confined to a wheelchair; but you cannot fix your own bad hip.

What in the world is the problem now? You once again begin to doubt.

The Elephant in the Room

Brothers and sisters, I tell you the truth; this thinking and the situation that I have described in the last few pages is more common than you may think. In fact, I dare say that *most* Christians feel this way or have experienced this type of thinking and feeling to a certain extent.

The problem is that you will be hard pressed to find anyone who will openly admit this. The very idea of admitting that you are in doubt, by itself, seems to make it so.

Who will admit that deep down inside they feel that things have not happened for them or that most of their prayers have not been answered?

Who will openly admit that they feel that God has not blessed them? Who will tell you that they are tired; they are tired of praying and waiting and waiting and praying? You will not hear such a thing from most Christians. Instead, when asked how things are going for them, the response is more likely to be,

"I am blessed and highly favored!"

The question is what is wrong? Why do so many of us suffer and do not see the miraculous blessing and favor of God on a regular basis?

You may not have had a continuous struggle as described above, but chances are that you have been there. Chances are, if you are reading this book, that you know what I mean.

Maybe it is only one thing, just one thing that you have been praying for forever that will just not come to pass.

What is wrong? Is the Bible wrong? Is the Word of God wrong? Good heavens, no! We know that the Word of God is correct. We know that the Word of God is immutable, indisputable and absolutely irrefutable! It is clear that the Word says things like...

"I can do all things through Christ which strengtheneth me"
---Philippians 4:13(KJV)

"And whatsoever ye shall ask in my name, that will I do, that the Father may be glorified in the Son. If ye shall ask any thing in my name, I will do it."
---John 14:13-14(KJV)

"Delight thyself also in the Lord: and he shall give thee the desires of thine heart."
---Psalm 37:4(KJV)

"Give, and it will be given to you. They will pour into your lap a good measure, pressed down, shaken together, and running over..."
---Luke 6:38(KJV)

"Beloved, I wish above all things that thou mayest prosper and be in health, even as thy soul prospereth."

--- 3 John 1:2(KJV)

"Who his own self bare our sins in his own body on the tree, that we, being dead to sins, should live unto righteousness: by whose stripes ye were healed."

---1 Peter 2:24(KJV)

My Word! Do you hear what I say? Must I go on? Can you say, *"By His stripes we were healed?"* In Jesus name, His Word is truth. We know this.

So, then what is wrong? How come so many of us are not witnessing the glory of God and basking in the glow of His righteousness?

Some Christians are so tired that they have just given in and resigned themselves to a life of struggle, stress and strife. We see this especially in the older generation, the *Silent Generation*. So many saints sit back and welcome a life of poverty and want, in lieu of great blessing and favor that they have now decided they will only see *by and by*.

They talk about being so glad to, *"just make it in…"* All I want to do is make it in…to heaven that is.

14

They wait on the reward that God promised when we leave this world, when we get to heaven.

But Jesus said that He came not only so that we have life (everlasting), but that we may have it more abundantly! That is life in the here and now!

So just what is the problem and what is the answer? Get a pen, a highlighter or whatever, because right now I am going to tell you exactly what is wrong.

The Answer

The answer, the key to everything and every problem you have ever had is so simple that it eludes most of us. It is so plain that we miss it.

The answer to walking and living a life in the Divine consciousness of God's glorious righteousness is exactly that:

The Consciousness of Righteousness.

We do not live in the consciousness of righteousness. The manifestation of all your prayers and the answer to living the favor of God till your cup runneth over, is simply living in the consciousness of righteousness.

Let me say this to begin; this is not a new thing or a crazy theory or some cult-like, metaphysical or psychological nonsense.

The idea of living in the state of the consciousness of God's righteousness comes directly from the Bible. It is scripture and has been there since the beginning. Over the next few chapters, I am going to explain to you exactly how and show you where in the Bible you can live in the consciousness of righteousness starting as soon as tomorrow.

As soon as next week, tomorrow or by the time you finish reading the last page in this book, you will be witnessing the greatest breakthrough of your lifetime.

Are you ready? Then let's get to it!

CHAPTER 1
The Overview

Yes, by the time you finish this book, you will be on the other side of the greatest breakthrough in your life.

You will no longer need to pray and wait and wait and pray for a healing; you will walk in divine health!

You will not have to beg and plead with the Lord for a financial windfall. You will live in the glory of the King, just like a king! It will be poured out into your lap; good measure, pressed down, shaken together, and running over! Everything you touch will prosper, even as your soul prospers!

So let's get to it. First, let me give you an overview of how we will go about this and how the book lays it out.

Starting in the next chapter, we will get into what the consciousness of righteousness means. Exactly what is the consciousness of righteousness? How do we obtain it?   How do we *live* the consciousness of righteousness?

However, in explaining what it means to live in the consciousness of righteousness, it is best first to describe the *opposite* of this consciousness. That is, to explain what it is to *not* live in the consciousness of righteousness, because this is a position that we can all very easily relate to and understand.

So, I will first talk about how most of us live right now, before we discover the consciousness of righteousness. We will go over the state of consciousness that most of us live in today and every day.

How did we get to this place, this level or condition of consciousness and this philosophy and thinking? Why do we continue in this awareness, this cognizance? We will get deep into such questions and look at what the Bible tells us about them, including how it all started.

Then, I will explain and define the consciousness of righteousness and we will examine a ton of scripture on the subject.

Good Lord, we will get deep into this and I believe the Holy Spirit will enlighten you. You will see that the consciousness of righteousness is nothing new and nothing secret, it is actually basic scripture. In fact, it is so fundamental that it is easy for us to look right past it. Of course, we also have the devil standing in the wings, helping to misdirect us from this simple truth, as well.

This simple truth is so basic that we by pass it. It is so natural to the born again Christian that it is nearly intrinsic, inherent to your salvation. It is the foundation of the very gospel of Jesus Christ!

Not only is the consciousness of righteousness so simple, foundational and clear in the Word of God that we usually overlook it, but we also do not remember it. It is easy for us to forget (also with a little help from the devil).

However, we will delve deep into the Word of God on the consciousness of righteousness and then I will give you a clear and easy to remember acronym to help you keep all of what you learn about righteousness nature and thinking, at the very forefront of your mind. Remember this acronym and you will remember the precise process to maintain the consciousness of righteousness.

Then, to help you maintain and better digest this Word from the Lord, I provide a short *review* at the end of each chapter with five bullet points highlighting the key ideas from the chapter. You will find that months or even years after you read this book; you can come back and go over those *Key Consciousness Points* for an instant refresher course.

Finally, I will offer an impartation prayer at the end of the chapter that will also help you reinforce and seal the ideas of that chapter into your body, mind and spirit.

Once you are able to maintain the consciousness of righteousness, once you are able simply to walk in the mind and awareness, once it becomes second nature to you, it will transform your life.

Living in the consciousness of righteousness will be such a transformative breakthrough for you that it will transform and affect those around you. You will glow with the glory of God and perform miracles greater than that of Jesus Himself. The Bible tells us this:

"Verily, verily, I say unto you, He that believeth on me, the works that I do he shall do also; and greater works than these shall he do; because I go unto my Father."

---John 12:12(KJV)

You, yes, I am talking to you reading this book right now, whoever you are; you will do greater miracles than Jesus did.

Let me share a short story with you that I think perfectly illustrates the consciousness of righteousness. I like stories and you will find many of them as you read this book. Some are analogies, parables if you will, that help explain a point. Yet some are true stories, testimonies of several people that I have helped come into the clarity of the consciousness of righteousness. In their own words, they will tell you the incredible change it made in their lives. You will hear of their struggles and trials in their Christian walk until they came to a righteousness nature.

But first, here is a short tale that I think will help set up and establish the idea of what the consciousness of righteousness is and the revelation that awaits you.

A Long Trip to the Promised Land

Please imagine if you will, that it is way back around the late 1930s' and we are far off in a distance country. The time is just before World War II.

We have been so fortunate here in America as to not have had a major war on our soil, in our lifetime. Praise God! But as you can imagine, that could not be an easy thing to go through.

Can you imagine tanks and air raids happening right in your neighborhood? Can you imagine troops with machine guns and grenade launchers taking over the local Walmart, using it as a base?

War tears a country apart. The devastation that war leaves behind we label as a *war-torn* country. So, imagine we are in war-torn Europe somewhere and it is bad; people being killed, homes, businesses raided and bombed, it's a real bad time. People are trying to escape, trying to find a way out of certain death.

Now, down near the ocean front, at the docks, there is a great big boat that is about to leave for the United Stated of America. The boat is going to a safe place, and everybody wants to get on that boat to America.

People heard of the great country; they heard of that country of freedom. They heard that there was no war in America, only peace, and everyone wanted to get on that boat to the land of the free.

However, it was a private boat, reserved only for the select people of the royal family. No one else could even get near the boat. The royal guards, heavily armed with machine guns, stood at the pier stopping people from getting on. They would shoot to kill anyone who attempted to get on that boat who was not a member of the royal family or their servants.

They did have some servants; butlers, maids and workers who could get on board; and no, they were not taking applications for any of those positions at the time.

To get on that boat, you had to have a special ticket that identified you as a worker in the royal household. It didn't matter how much money you had, or what your status was, you couldn't work for a ticket or buy a ticket.

Now there was this young man who like tons of other people, ran to the dock in an effort to get on the boat to America, but once he saw the mobs of people, some jumping in the water, fighting, scratching, clawing, and getting shot, he knew it was hopeless. He just turned around with his head down and started to walk away.

Well there was another young man who was on the boat. He was not dressed very fancy; in fact, he looked like he was probably one of the royal family's servants. But he was on the boat and noticed the man afar off, walking away, dejected. So, this servant fellow came down off of the boat. He pushed his way through the crowds and caught up with the saddened young man who was walking away.

He came up to him and he said, "I have decided and have chosen to remain here to see if I can help save more people. I want you to take my place on the boat. I want to exchange places with you. Take my ticket and enjoy everything that comes with it...here, it's yours."

"Whaaaat?!" The dejected man was shocked. He thought it had to be some sort of a trick or something. He says, "Wait a minute...I mean, I can't pay you for this ticket and you don't even know me and you mean to tell me that you are going to just *give* me your ticket, and you are going to stay here and probably die? I don't understand..."

The man stopped him and said, "Look, we can stand here and debate this, or you can just take the ticket. It's a gift to you. You can either accept it or reject it. But that boat is leaving in about two minutes, so it's your choice, what do you want to do?"

Well, of course, the man says, "Well this doesn't make any sense, but I'll take it! Thank you! Thank you so much!" He runs through the crowd holding up that ticket yelling, "Hold that boat...I've got a ticket!" He gets on the boat and the boat leaves for the land of the free.

Well, it was only a few minutes into the voyage that he realized something; he did not have a dime. He didn't have any food, clothes or anything. He had nothing and those trips were long back then. It was not like these big ships today...no, no. This trip was going to takes a couple of months and he didn't have anything but the clothes on his back.

But, he didn't care. He thought, "As long as I'm on the boat, as long as I get there...that's all that matters. I may starve half way to death...but as long as I make it in, that's all that counts."

And he did nearly starve to death. His sleeping quarters was down in steerage; third class, the bottom of the boat and his bunk was literally in the mist of the huge boiler. But that didn't faze him.

He found a bag of peanuts and for a while he would eat just two or three peanuts a day. That's all he ate, a couple peanuts a day. Then he began to go up on the fancy lido deck where the rich people would hang out near the swimming pool, but he would wait until after it got dark and no one was out there. Then he would go and scrounge around to see what scraps he could find and what leftovers people discarded as garbage. He did whatever he had to do, whatever it took, *anything* just to make it there. Well, he did make it there. He survived. He made it to America.

He came off the boat, barely walking. He was so malnourished, frail and weak that he could hardly stand. Trembling and shaking as he walked, he just collapsed and fell to the ground. There, lying prone in the street, he kissed the ground.

Just then, a gentleman came up and began to assist him. This man was obviously part of the royal family as he had on an expensive looking suit with tails and he wore a top hat. Helping the man to his knees, he asked, "Son, are you ok? Are you alright?"

The man, still on his knees, looked up with a great big smile and said, "Oh yes! I am just fine! Yes I am ok...I am ok NOW! Because I'm here, I am finally here! I made it! Thank God, I made it!"

The man in tails looked down at him and said, "Yes, yes, I see." Then he stopped and stared at the half-starved man for a moment, apparently recognizing him.

"You know, I've seen you before, haven't I?" the rich man asked. "Weren't you on the boat that just came in from the war area?"

"Yes! Yes I was." The thin starved man proudly proclaimed.

"You know," the top hat said, "I wondered about you. I knew I had seen you once or twice, but I realized that I never saw you up in the dining area. I never saw you up on deck. How come you never came up to dine with us?"

"Oh no, no. You misunderstand." He said. "You see, I was on the boat, true. But my ticket was for down in the steerage area, third-class. My ticket was for the lower decks; my cabin was on the bottom floor, near the boiler."

Steadying himself, he continued.

"I didn't have first-class accommodations or anything like that, and I didn't have any money...so I was happy to just stay in my cabin for the most of the journey."

"Oh, my." The rich guy said. "I'm so sorry to hear that."

"No...no! Don't be sorry for me. I'm glad! I made it---that's all that counts."

"No, that's not what I meant when I said I'm sorry." The top hat said. "I mean, I'm sorry that you didn't know."

"Uh?" The starving man said as he rose to his feet, a bewildered look now griped his face. "I didn't know what?"

The rich man, hung his head and said, "I'm sorry to tell you but the tickets, yes they determined your cabin area, they determined where you slept. And yes, there were Royal cabins and first-class and second class and so on, but that was just for your cabin."

He continued, "But you see, son, every ticket, every single ticket, no matter what class the ticket was, with every ticket came with it…all the food you could eat!

All the food you could possibly eat and all of the amenities on the boat were all yours to enjoy. You see son, everything on the boat was included in your ticket.

All the meals you wanted, 24 hours a day, 7 days a week; full buffets with all the trimmings, everything was yours. It was all available to you. We had turkey, fish, caviar, shrimp and lobster and chicken and ribs, and anything you can think of. All you had to do was come up and claim it!

From tea to lemonade to fruit punch and the finest champagne, it all came with your ticket!

You could have also used the gym and worked out, took a swim in the pool or did some jogging around the lido deck. You could have stretched out on one of the long lounge chairs and bathed in the sun. You could have taken a soothing steam bath or had a relaxing message.

Remember son, this boat was only for members of the royal family, not strangers. Everyone on the boat was heir to the royal throne, including the servants. Son, *everything* you ever wanted or needed came with your ticket. With your ticket you were part of the family, it was your right. It was already available to you and it was in the palm of your hand."

Oh my God! Can you see what I am saying? Now I can spend hours on this story, but let me just make one thing clear as to how it relates to us and the revelation of the consciousness of righteousness.

Everything is Included with Your Ticket!

You can see the obvious in that at salvation, we can often be so grateful just to make it into heaven that we sit and wait for the end of the journey without reaping all of the rewards that are available to us *along* the journey.

However, Jesus said that He came that you have life and have it more abundantly. So yes, we need to take everything else in; all that comes along with the ticket of salvation. With our ticket to heaven comes so much more; more blessings that we can reap and enjoy in the here and now, today.

Often we live on a few peanuts a day, while all the time the buffet is open and available to us! It all comes with your ticket!

Do you hear what I say? Good Lord, hallelujah! I am trying to make this short, but I keep shouting in between writing! Let me calm down.

Listen; here is the question for you. What did the man on the boat have to do to gain all of the things he ever wanted or needed on the boat?

What would he have had to do to take advantage of everything that was available to him?

Would he have had to develop a new skill? No.

Would he have had to learn and study to be able to get the things that he needed and wanted? No.

Would he have had to pay anything or invest something or trade something? No.

Exactly what did he have to do in order to reap all of the rewards that were available to him on the boat?

Hear me now. This is important.

All he had to do was understand who he was and the true value of what he already had.

All he had to do was truly understand who he really was. He thought that all he was, was a third-class, steerage passenger with no rights, rewards or benefits.

But he found out that he was a passenger who was a part of the royal family and who was entitled to all of the benefits of anyone on the boat. He had all the rights and all of the rewards, all of the benefits of the royal family!

All he had to do was *understand* who he was and what he had!

Listen now. All he had to do was *become aware* of what he had. All he had to do was *become conscious* of what he already had!

He lived in the consciousness of steerage. He lived in the consciousness of a third-class life. While in this consciousness, it was impossible for anything to change. He could not live beyond his own consciousness. He could not live beyond his own thinking. You cannot live beyond your thinking.

However, if he had become aware of the truth, if he had come into the consciousness of royalty, can you see how it would have changed everything?

All it took was for him to live in the consciousness of his royal-ness and everything would change.

You might be thinking that it would have been nice if someone had only told him what he had and that everything was included. But someone did.

When the servant came off the boat and gave him the ticket, he said exactly this,

"...Take my ticket and enjoy everything that comes with it...here, it's yours."

Enjoy everything that comes with it. He was so elated about getting on the boat, the young man overlooked that simple statement and he never remembered it. He never even asked the simple, obvious question, "What comes with it?"

That is a good representation of us. That is exactly where most of us are when it comes to the consciousness of righteousness.

The Lord told us, He gave us the key to living in the consciousness of His royalty in many places in the Bible. But it is so subtle, so simple that we overlook it.

You do not need to learn something new. You do not need to become a Bible scholar. You do not need to become a saint.

All you need do is come to the understanding and realization of who you really are and what you already have; and that, my friends, is what this book is all about.

I am going to systematically help you see and realize who you are and what you already have.

Once you understand, once you see it and realize it, that's it! It will change everything!

Once you come to *live* in the consciousness of righteousness, the buffet is open!

Key Consciousness Points - Chapter 1
The Overview

1. At salvation, many people are so overjoyed at the prospect of having eternal life in Heaven, that they overlook most of the additional benefits of salvation.

2. Those key benefits include the overabundance of life, joy, happiness and prosperity right here today, during our life on Earth.

3. Many spend a lifetime working harder, praying more vigorously and performing better to gain the skills to manifest the power of God.

4. It does not have anything to do with working harder or performing better, nor do you have to learn new skills. It has nothing to do with what you do.

5. All you need is to become aware, become conscious of who you are and what you already have.

Impartation Prayer

Dear Father,

I sincerely thank you for the whole package of salvation; it is complete and there is nothing missing in it. Who could come up with a better plan to restore me so totally, than you? Thank you my Lord!

Just like sin entered our lives through Adam and spoiled the entire world, Jesus Your holy Son, restored the entire world, restored all the saints to righteousness, including me.

I thank You Lord as I know I did nothing to help in the work You did on the cross, and likewise my performance can have no effect on that work. Now I am confident that I am forever restored by the death and resurrection of Your Holy Son, Jesus, and I am righteous to the end. Amen! I love you father!

CHAPTER 2

What is the
Consciousness of Righteousness?

As I mentioned, to better explain what the consciousness of righteousness is, it is best first to explain and explore what it is *not*.

One thing that the consciousness of righteousness is not is something that you do. It is not something that you do, nor something that you learn. The consciousness of righteousness is not about how much or how many scriptures you know by heart.

It is not about your performance. No. It is not about how charitable you are or how much you help the homeless or feed the poor or how morally upright you are. The consciousness of righteousness is also not about how much self-control you have and how much you avoid sin.

It is not even about how well you know the Bible or your level or position in ministry or in the church. The consciousness of righteousness is not about getting your Doctorates in Theology. No, no, no.

Believe me; I thought such things had to do with righteousness too. When I looked at my life and found that I too, was in that up and down, whirlpool cycle of going from strong belief, to seeing things nothing happen, to doubt and discouragement, to justification, repentance, and back to strong belief again, I knew something was wrong.

Yes, I was there too, praying and waiting and waiting and praying. After 29 years of active, enthusiastic ministry in the church, I had to painfully admit that I was still empty inside. I was not full of the joy of Christ and my cup did not runneth over.

After nearly three decades of dedication and commitment to the Word of God, I had to face the truth, which was that I was still weak, powerless and tired. Jesus, I was so, so tired.

I was still thoroughly conscious of sin. In fact, I was conscious *only* of sin. During that time, like many of you, I did what I thought would satisfy my needs and answer my prayers.

I prayed more and worked harder. I received the baptism of the Holy Spirit. I also did not learn about *fire baptism* until later in my Christian walk and of course, I thought that it was the missing element. It was not.

Then I went to theology school and began to learn as much as I could of the Word. This had to be the answer. But no, it was not.

I became a preacher and set out singlehandedly to complete the Great Commission and preach the Word *to the ends of the earth*!

Still, sin consciousness engulfed me. Like that man on the boat in the story earlier, I could only think in terms of a third-class passenger. I was only aware of, I was only conscious of, sin and trying to overcome and avoid it. Sin and therefore, the law, ruled my thoughts as it does most of us. It was a constant performance battle of trying to *do* better.

Then one day, one glorious day, it hit me. The Holy Spirit washed me with a word, one word: "consciousness."

I wasn't exactly sure why the Lord put this word on my heart nor was I exactly sure of even what it meant. But for the next few weeks I could not escape this word, *consciousness.*

Of course, I began to do some research. I looked up the word and found nothing too surprising in the basic meaning.

As I thought, it simply means awareness or being aware.

Merriam-Webster.com

Consciousness: noun

> "1a: the quality or state of being aware especially of something within oneself.
>
> b: the state or fact of being conscious of an external object, state, or fact
>
> c: awareness; especially: concern for some social or political cause…"

Right, like I said. Then I looked a little closer into the definition and found the word *awake.* Uhm. Being awake. I thought about Adam and how when God breathed the *breath of life* into Adam's nostrils, he became a living soul; he became awake. Okay, I was onto something, but I still wasn't sure of exactly what.

So, as any diligent Biblical researcher would do, I then looked up the word in the Greek and found some revelation knowledge.

The word consciousness translated back to the Greek comes from the word, *suneidon* or *suneidésis;* a combination of the words, *syn* and *eidō,* which, in English means, *"to know"* or *"to see."* It means *joint-knowing,* joined knowledge, a shared knowledge.

An intimate shared knowledge, the result of being created in the image of the Almighty God!

Strong's Concordance 4893

syneídēsis (from 4862 /*sýn,*"together *with"* and 1492 /*eídō* "to know, see") – properly, joint-knowing, i.e. *conscience* which joins moral and spiritual consciousness as part of being created in the divine image. Accordingly, *all* people have this God-given capacity to know right from wrong because each is a *free moral agent.*

Good Lord! Are your seeing this? All people have this. All people have this innate knowledge, shared with God, as to internal decrement of right and wrong, good and evil.

Studying this down a bit further, I found that this consciousness can lean one of two ways:

Thayer's Greek Lexicon

a. the consciousness of _anything_: a soul conscious of sins, or

b. the consciousness of _nobility_; a soul mindful of its noble origin

My God, my God!

We have this shared knowledge, but somewhere along the way, it turned to focus only on that consciousness of _anything_, the consciousness of sin. Our focus, our entire awareness and state of being awake, all centers around sin.

I began to think, "What happened to the consciousness of nobility? What happened to having the mind of our noble and righteous origin?

That is when the Holy Spirit laid another word on my heart, _righteousness_. And it all started to become clear.

Merriam-Webster's Definition of Righteous

1: acting in accord with divine or moral law free from guilt or sin

2 a: morally right or justifiable *a righteous decision*

b: arising from an outraged sense of justice or morality *righteous indignation*

3 *slang*: genuine, excellent

Strong's Concordance: Righteous 1343

dikaiosýnē (from 1349 /*díkē*, "a judicial verdict") properly, *judicial approval* (the *verdict* of *approval*); in the NT, *the approval* of God ("divine approval")

To be righteous is to be as pure as the driven snow, without blemish; free from guilt or sin. The verdict is in and it is the absolute Divine approval of the Holiness of God Himself!

Righteousness; therein is the origin of our nobility. Righteousness; therein is the origin, the essence of what we are. Righteousness is the foundation of what we are. Righteousness is the state, the condition in which we are born again. We are *born* righteous! We are born the Righteousness of God!

Right then, instantly things began to change for me. I still had not put this whole understanding together where I could talk to other people about it. I still had not put it all together in my own head yet. But just by grasping that little piece, just starting to understand the concept of having the consciousness, the awareness, the state of being awake and having the shared knowledge of God of our righteousness; that alone was a revelation.

The realization that I, like the Lord Jesus, the Christ Himself, am as pure, as sinless, as Holy as He is; that I too am righteous, began to change me.

Just by beginning to understand that we have the shared state of being righteous, that we are indeed righteous from spiritual birth; began to have a miraculous effect on my life.

Right away, my thinking changed. I no longer thought of or focused on sin. I just did not think about it anymore. I didn't even think about lying or cheating or sexual sin.

I had struggled daily for years with selfishness in the past. Now, I just never thought about it anymore. It just never came to my mind.

And do you know what happened? The instant I stopped thinking about those sins, they stopped! Do you hear what I say?

The sins just stopped, or should I say, I stopped committing them. After a week of this thinking, of righteousness thinking, I noticed that the things that I struggled with and usually focused on avoiding, once I stopped being mindful of them, they just faded away.

I also noticed that many things that used to worry me silly, didn't even come to mind anymore. I tell you, there were problems that I had and issues that I knew were on their way, and suddenly I found that I couldn't even remember what they were.

My God, what was happening? I had to learn more.

Living the Consciousness of Righteousness

I was in a state of euphoria, a kind of high. I guess you could call it a state of *heightened awareness*. I began to understand that I needed to stay right here, right where I was. I realized that if I could stay in this constant state of thinking, in this state of consciousness forever, that would be it, the answer to all my prayers.

Good Lord, if I could only maintain this consciousness of righteousness, it would change everything! And that was it. I had to *live* the consciousness of righteousness. It had to become my way of thinking, my *only* way of thinking.

Philippians 3:9

Although I had known this verse for years, it started to make more sense to me now.

"And be found in him, not having mine own righteousness, which is of the law, but that which is through the faith of Christ, the righteousness which is of God by faith:"
---Philippians 3:9(KJV)

As I said earlier, it is not about anything that you do or learn to do or having any specific skill. It is about you putting on the righteousness of God through your faith in Christ.

It is not about you becoming better. In fact, it is not really about you, period. It is about Christ. It is about Christ living inside of you.

Christ is righteous. Christ is our righteousness and He lives in you, (that are saved) and the Bible is loaded with scriptures that confirm this.

"In his days Judah shall be saved, and Israel shall dwell safely: and this is his name whereby he shall be called, The Lord Our Righteousness."
---Jeremiah 23:6(KJV)

"For therein is the righteousness of God revealed from faith to faith: as it is written, The just shall live by faith."

---Romans 1:17(KJV)

"In those days, and at that time, will I cause the Branch of righteousness to grow up unto David; and he shall execute judgment and righteousness in the land."

---Jeremiah 33:15(KJV)

You have to remember what actually happened on the Cross at Calvary. Christ died for our sins. Yes, He did...thank you Jesus!

But He also took our place. He traded places with us. He exchanged places with us. He *took* our sin and gave us His righteousness!

"For he hath made him to be sin for us, who knew no sin; that we might be made the righteousness of God in him."

---2 Corinthians 5:21(KJV)

We already have it. We were born again with it. We *are* it! And now we have to learn to *live* it! That is *live* it. Not pray for it, or work to get it, or do it. Just live it.

I think that's going to be my new slogan. There is Nike's famous, "Just do it." Well how about, *"Just LIVE It!"*

The Consciousness of Righteousness: *Just LIVE it!*

But what does that mean? What does it mean to just live it? Let's go back to our story and the man on the boat.

While the man did not know that everything on the boat was included and he could have anything he wanted, he suffered. He had everything and the rights to everything that he ever wanted, but he still struggled. He lived a continuous struggle of starving, stress and strife.

He woke up every day, praying. He would pray that God help him find food for another day. He prayed harder and more often. Sometimes it seemed his prayers were answered and sometimes they were not. He lived in a state of constant struggle, but he continued to pray and wait and wait and pray.

Does that sound familiar? Is that not exactly what we do?

He prayed for help, but could God answer those prayers? No! Could God answer his prayer for food? No, because He already answered those prayers! God had already given him everything he needed; he just was not aware of it, he was not conscious of it.

Have you prayed and prayed and waited and prayed for something and it seemed like God would not answer?

Actually, it may be that God had already answered the need, solved the issue and provided the solution, long before you even knew you had a problem and ever prayed the prayer! Thank you Jesus!

Now think about this. What if the man on the boat had become aware of what he had? What if he became conscious of the fact that he had the rights to everything on the boat?

Here is the question. I really need you to get this.

If he had become conscious that everything was included on the boat, would he have had to pray for food?

Would he wake up every morning, praying that God help him find food for another day?

No! Of course not! Why would he need to pray and ask for something that he already had? That wouldn't make any sense.

He would not have been praying and waiting and waiting and praying. He would not have been struggling.

Would he have had to concentrate or focus on eating? Honestly, he wouldn't even have had to ever *think* about eating!

Are you with me?

Our hero always thought about one thing--- eating. He had the consciousness of finding food and living for another day.

But once he knew what he had; once he developed a consciousness of what was available to him, more than likely, he would not have thought about eating and surviving again! He would just live it!

It's one thing to say, "I know there is that terrible virus going around, but I have faith that I will not get it. I will not get sick, in the name of Jesus!"

Okay, that's good. Amen. However, it is still an acknowledgment of the virus and acceptance to the fact that the virus can make you sick. There is still thought of the virus.

However, it is an entirely different matter to say, "What virus? What are you talking about?"

Good God, do you hear what I say?

You have big school exam coming up soon. This one test can mean the difference in you getting into college or not. You can pray,

"Father, in the name of Jesus, I ask that you take over. Holy Spirit, guide my mind and bring all things back to my remembrance so that I pass this test…"

Okay. There's nothing really bad about that. However, can you see the acknowledgement and acceptance that there is the real possibility of not passing the exam?

Alternatively, you can pray,

"Father, I thank you in advance for the victory! I know that I will not fail this test. I know that it is your will that I go to college, in the name of Jesus…"

Amen! That's stronger. That's faith, right? That's claiming it. But again, the thought is still on failure. However, what about this...

Before the exam, you have already packed your clothes, ordered books and put in a change of address at the post office because the thought of *not* passing the exam ***never even crossed your mind!***

That's living it!

JUST LIVE IT!

Key Consciousness Points - Chapter 2

What is the

Consciousness of Righteousness?

1. The consciousness of righteousness is not about you. It is about Christ. It is about Christ living in you.

2. Consciousness is a joint-awareness shared by you and God. Consciousness can be of sin or of righteousness.

3. Righteousness is the Holy and sin free purity of the almighty God the Father. You are the righteousness of God through your faith in Christ Jesus.

4. We have to turn from our consciousness of sin and become aware of our consciousness of righteousness.

5. Then we need to live in that state of being. We must live the consciousness of righteousness.

Impartation Prayer

Dear Father,

How do I exalt Your name for this great revelation knowledge that comes my way today? My righteousness is not about me but about Christ living in me. May Christ show Himself visible in every way in my life and my world!

May this revelation knowledge continue to burn in every part of my mind and my body until it consumes my entire being forever! I truly bless Your name with all my heart because You are the one who has freed me from all my unrighteousness.

Once again, oh Lord, I thank you for being so wonderful towards me. Amen!

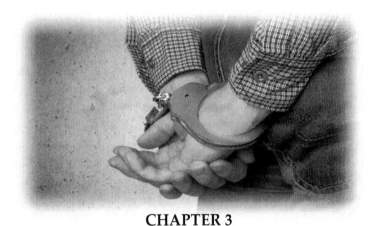

CHAPTER 3

Adam and Eve and
The Origin of Sin Consciousness

I hope that everything in the last chapter is clear to you. If not, please read it again. It is vitally important that you understand this. If you are having a problem understanding it, then you are probably over thinking it.

It is actually very simple. The simplicity of the consciousness of righteousness is the very reason why almost all of us missed it. We have bought into the devil's fabricated view of the Bible and scripture that it is so complicated and hard to understand.

We have to try always to keep in mind that Biblical understanding is not intellectual or even logical; it is spiritual.

So, we know that we, once born again, *are* the righteousness of God. We do not have to get it, we are it. We need simply to become aware of it, conscious of it, and then live it or actualize it.

We also know that there are two forms of consciousness. There is the consciousness of sin and the consciousness of righteousness. We naturally live the consciousness of sin and we need to change to live the consciousness of righteousness.

This brings up a good question. How did we get here? How did we get to this place of living in a consciousness of sin? What ever happened to the consciousness of nobility, the consciousness of righteousness from the day we are born again? Why do we not automatically turn to the consciousness of righteousness when we are born again?

Those are very good questions. For the answer to those questions, we can look to the very first two people God ever created.

Adam and Eve: Born Righteous

When we go back to the beginning, that is the very beginning, we see that what happened with our righteousness is very clear.

First, we have to remember that Adam and Eve were originally born perfect. They were born without blemish, without sin and had eternal life. They were born Holy and directly connected to God. They were born righteous. They were born the righteousness of God.

"And God said, Let us make man in our image, after our likeness: and let them have dominion over the fish of the sea, and over the fowl of the air, and over the cattle, and over all the earth, and over every creeping thing that creepeth upon the earth.

So God created man in his own image, in the image of God created he him; male and female created he them."
---Genesis 1:26–27(KJV)

They were born in the direct image of the Almighty Creator, including His holiness and righteousness.

God then gave them dominion to rule over all the earth. God gave Adam and Eve control over everything that He had just created.

"And God blessed them, and God said unto them, Be fruitful, and multiply, and replenish the earth, and subdue it: and have dominion over the fish of the sea, and over the fowl of the air, and over every living thing that moveth upon the earth.

And God said, Behold, I have given you every herb bearing seed, which is upon the face of all the earth, and every tree, in the which is the fruit of a tree yielding seed; to you it shall be for meat.

And to every beast of the earth, and to every fowl of the air, and to every thing that creepeth upon the earth, wherein there is life, I have given every green herb for meat: and it was so.

And God saw every thing that he had made, and, behold, it was very good. And the evening and the morning were the sixth day."

---Genesis 1:28–31(KJV)

Adam and Eve had all power and only one way of thinking; one way of living, one consciousness which was the consciousness of righteousness. They had no thought of sin. They were not even aware of sin. God gave them everything that they would ever need and Adam and Eve were able to just chill out with no worries and not a care in the world.

They had no knowledge of sin and God wanted to keep it that way. He told them not to eat from the one tree that would give them the knowledge and awareness of sin.

"And the Lord God commanded the man, saying, Of every tree of the garden thou mayest freely eat:

But of the tree of the knowledge of good and evil, thou shalt not eat of it: for in the day that thou eatest thereof thou shalt surely die."

---Genesis 2: 16-17(KJV)

God told Adam that if he tasted or learned from the tree of knowledge of Good and Evil, that all Hell would break loose, and that is exactly what happened.

Once Adam and Eve became aware of sin, they then began to focus on sin. Once the knowledge of sin entered into their thinking, they immediately focused on sin and withdrew from God.

"And when the woman saw that the tree was good for food, and that it was pleasant to the eyes, and a tree to be desired to make one wise, she took of the fruit thereof, and did eat, and gave also unto her husband with her; and he did eat.

And the eyes of them both were opened, and they knew that they were naked; and they sewed fig leaves together, and made themselves aprons.

And they heard the voice of the Lord God walking in the garden in the cool of the day: and Adam and his wife hid themselves from the presence of the Lord God amongst the trees of the garden."

---Genesis 3: 6-8(KJV)

They were fine. They were just going about their business, basking and frolicking in the Garden and they were naked the whole time.

Once the thought of sin and evil came to mind, they immediately began to judge themselves in the sight of God.

When you have the thought of sin, a mindset of sin, and then come into the presence and holiness of God, the natural reaction is to recoil in shame and fear. The natural response is to pull away from God.

Again, at first, Adam and Eve had no thoughts of sin, and while they had no thoughts of sin, everything was fine and they did not sin.

Let me say that again. While they had no thought, no awareness, no consciousness of sin, they did not sin and had no fear or shame. Wow. Do you hear what I say?

Is it starting to sink in yet? Remember what happened with me. Once I began to realize that I was born the righteousness of God and started to focus less on sin, I sinned less.

While I focused on trying to avoid sin and trying not to do this and that, it was a constant struggle. But once I began to focus on righteousness and forgot about sin, I had peace.

Once I shifted my thoughts from a consciousness of sin to a consciousness of righteousness, I had power. This too, is one of the many things that the Bible told us to do. The scriptures make it clear that we need to stop focusing on sin and focus only on righteousness, only on Christ and we will have total power and peace, and everything that we need.

"Thou wilt keep him in perfect peace, whose mind is stayed on thee: because he trusteth in thee."

---Isaiah 26:3(KJV)

The Amplified Version breaks this verse down a little more for you

"You will keep in perfect and constant peace the one whose mind is steadfast [that is, committed and focused on You —in both inclination and character], Because he trusts and takes refuge in You [with hope and confident expectation].

---Isaiah 26:3(AMP)

If we keep our focus only on Him, only on gaining a closer walk with Him, everything else falls into place.

"But seek ye first the kingdom of God, and his righteousness; and all these things shall be added unto you."

---Matthew 6:33(KJV)

Righteousness Lost

Of course, it is not just about *thinking*. There was sin, a transgression that caused the problem. There was an event, an offence that caused Adam and Eve to lose their righteousness.

They disobeyed God's direct instruction, lost their righteousness standing and received punishment.

"Unto the woman he said, I will greatly multiply thy sorrow and thy conception; in sorrow thou shalt bring forth children; and thy desire shall be to thy husband, and he shall rule over thee."

And unto Adam he said, Because thou hast hearkened unto the voice of thy wife, and hast eaten of the tree, of which I commanded thee, saying, Thou shalt not eat of it: cursed is the ground for thy sake; in sorrow shalt thou eat of it all the days of thy life;

Thorns also and thistles shall it bring forth to thee; and thou shalt eat the herb of the field; In the sweat of thy face shalt thou eat bread, till thou return unto the ground; for out of it wast thou taken: for dust thou art, and unto dust shalt thou return."

---Genesis 3:16-21(KJV)

Whoa. That's was pretty harsh, uh? Yes, Adam and Eve lost their righteousness standing (and consequently ours as well) and received a real whipping.

Here we see the introduction of menstrual cycles and other women's pain and problems concerning their reproductive system. Yes, ladies, you can blame all the cramps, mood swings and hot flashes on Eve.

Then God commanded men to work basically, until they die. And upon that death, our bodies now revert back to dust. No more immortality.

God also drove Adam and Eve out of the Garden, or actually, He moved them to another side of the Garden and blocked their way to the Tree of Life.

Many people believe this was also part of God's punishment. However, moving and preventing them access to the Tree of Life, was not punishment, actually it was a huge blessing. In fact, though I cannot get into this right now, that act is one of the single greatest blessings God ever bestowed on us.

Adam and Eve's sin did indeed sever that holy umbilical cord between humankind and God. They separated themselves from God. God did not push them away or move away or separate from them; they did it. Since then, all descendants of Adam and Eve are born *already* separated from God. That state of being separated from God, is called sin.

Committing Sin and the Condition of Sin

There is sin the verb, as in you committing a sin. That sin is the individual action in where you commit a transgression against God.

However, sin is also a condition; it is a state of being. To be separated from God is to be in a state of sin. Once Adam and Eve became separated from God, all of their offspring, us, are born already separated from God as well.

Therefore, when we are first born, we are born into a state of sin. This is how you are born into sin. Through Adam, *all* sin came into the world.

Righteousness Promised

So, there we were, humans that is, living in a pretty hopeless state. We are born already separated from God, into a state of sin. Our spirit is no longer connected to God and no longer holy and therefore sinful. We are born into sin, with a sinful nature and a consciousness of sin.

"Behold, I was shapen in iniquity; and in sin did
my mother conceive me."

---Psalm 51:5(KJV)

"I was brought forth in [a state of] wickedness; In sin my
mother conceived me [and from my beginning I,
too, was sinful]."

---Psalm 51:5(AMP)

So, there we were with this terrible sinful nature and God gave us the Law or what is better known as the Law of Moses, the Commandments. If you could keep these commandments, you would live a life holy enough for God to consider you righteous.

The problem was that it was and still is absolutely impossible to live by those commandants. In the history of the whole world, only one person was ever able to live a life and not violate one of the commandments and that is Jesus.

Incidentally, there were a lot more than just the *Ten Commandments*. Yes, there are a few more than ten. By most accounts there are 613 commandments, including the famous ten that God inscribed on the stone tablets. Some scholars and theologians believe that when you break those 613 down and consider the offshoots of each, the number of commandments is closer to a few thousand.

Either way, if you violated one commandment, just one, you were guilty of all of them. Imagine that; you get a speeding ticket and when you go to court, not only do they charge you with speeding, but also with bank robbery, murder, assault, rape, embezzlement, fraud and everything else. If guilty of one, you are guilty of all.

Also, most of the commandments are not as clear cut as *thou shalt not kill,* or *thou shalt not steal* and things like that.   For instance, according to Old Testament Law, it is a sin to wear a wool-blend pair of pants or a suit or shirt made of cotton and silk.

"Thou shalt not wear a garment of divers sorts, as of woollen and linen together."
---Deuteronomy 22:11(KJV)

You could be in violation of the law if you had a bowel movement on the Sabbath day. It simply was not humanly possible to keep the law, and that was not the purpose of the law.

The law was meant to help us realize that it was hopeless to try to keep the law. We could not, on our own, ever be good enough or moral enough to be holy in the eyes of God. The law helped humans to understand that there is only one way for us ever to regain righteousness, and that is through a savior. We had to have God save us and bestow His righteousness on us. And that is exactly what He did.

Well back in the Old Testament days, God constantly gave us messages that He would save us. The Lord told us that He would not leave us hopeless and that the day would come when He would send a savior and once again, rain His righteousness upon us.

"Sow to yourselves in righteousness, reap in mercy; break up your fallow ground: for it is time to seek the Lord, till he come and rain righteousness upon you."

---Hosea 10:12(KJV)

God promised that He would use individuals, regular people to help lead the way.

"In those days, and at that time, will I cause the Branch of righteousness to grow up unto David; and he shall execute judgment and righteousness in the land."

---Jeremiah 33:15(KJV)

The Lord made it clear to all those who would keep the faith that a savoir was on the way; our salvation was at hand and His righteousness would once again be in us.

"Thus saith the Lord, Keep ye judgment, and do justice: for my salvation is near to come, and my righteousness to be revealed."

---Isaiah 56:1(KJV)

Righteousness Preached

Then Christ, the Savior, was born! The Lord Jesus Christ came and our salvation was near. However, He was to first live the life, a perfect, sin free life, and then He would sacrifice Himself for us, exchanging our sin for His righteousness. While He walked the earth, Christ preached and taught what was to come. He told us what we needed to do to get back into that righteous standing.

"But seek ye first the kingdom of God, and his righteousness; and all these things shall be added unto you."

---Matthew 6:33(KJV)

"For the kingdom of God is not meat and drink; but righteousness, and peace, and joy in the Holy Ghost."

---Romans 14:17(KJV)

Righteousness Restored

Then, after Christ died for us and made that loving, substitutional atonement, He made salvation and righteousness available to us once again.

"For he hath made him to be sin for us, who knew no sin; that we might be made the righteousness of God in him."

---2 Corinthians 5:21(KJV)

"And if Christ be in you, the body is dead because of sin; but the Spirit is life because of righteousness."

---Romans 8:10(KJV)

Good gracious! Yes, the body, the flesh is dead; but if Christ be in you, you have a new spirit, a regenerated spirit that is life! The spirit is life why? Because of the righteousness of God.

Of course, it is all only through faith.

"For the promise, that he should be the heir of the world, was not to Abraham, or to his seed, through the law, but through the righteousness of faith."

---Romans 4:13(KJV)

Once you believe, through Jesus Christ, you have your righteousness the likes of Christ Himself. You become just as He is, with no distinction and able to do everything He did, and more.

"Even the righteousness of God which is by faith of Jesus Christ unto all and upon all them that believe: for there is no difference:"

---Romans 3:23(KJV)

"But to him that worketh not, but believeth on him that justifieth the ungodly, his faith is counted for righteousness."

---Romans 4:5(KJV)

"And be found in him, not having mine own righteousness, which is of the law, but that which is through the faith of Christ, the righteousness which is of God by faith:"

---Philippians 3:9(KJV)

Righteousness Now

Adam and Eve were born the righteousness of God. They sinned, lost righteousness and living in a state of sin, became sin conscious; a condition which they passed on to their entire lineage, the entire human race.

Then our Lord and Savior Jesus the Christ came and saved us, exchanging His righteousness with our sinful condition. Once again, once saved, once you are born again, you are the righteousness of God!

Once you latch on to the actual fact, once you realize exactly who you are and whose you are, once you get the idea deep down into your very soul, and accept the fact that you are the righteousness of God, that you are the mirror image of Jesus Christ, then you will live in the consciousness of righteousness. That is when everything will change for you and you will literally walk by faith.

Living the Consciousness of Righteousness

Since I have been conducting seminars and teaching classes on the basic concept of the *Consciousness of Righteousness*, I have had many people tell me about their experiences.

People have told me how, once they got it, once they finally understood what they already had, and whom they are and whose they are; how life changed for them. Here is one of those testimonies.

"Since starting the study on the Consciousness of Righteousness with Joseph, it has brought me to a place, or helped me to better see who I am and whose I am and the power that I can walk in because Jesus lives in me.

The whole thing reminded me that it was God's idea, not my idea, that I am the Righteousness. God arranged this, not me. And now I don't concentrate on if something happens, or if I do something that is outside of the will of God, that I stick to that sin, I hold on to it. I don't hold on to it anymore.

I know I don't have to hold on to it because in God's eyes I am holy, blameless, pure! I can't tell you how powerful that is. I mean, there are all those classes on self-esteem and how beautiful you are and so forth, but you don't even have to worry about that because once you know who you are in God, all that low self-esteem goes out the window.

Then you are different. You walk different. You can start walking in what God already put in you: peace, love, patience, all the fruits of the spirit.

Also, the sense of understanding just how much God loved me, I mean I always knew that God loved me, but I didn't know how much He loved me or how He thought of me from the beginning of the foundation and how He truly sees us as His sons and daughters.

I mean we are bought up hearing the old thing that we are sinners, you know; sinners saved by grace. So, when you made a mistake, you just couldn't forgive yourself, it had to be grace, God's grace. So you just kept holding on to it. Never really knowing deep down inside if you were straight with God.

But knowing and understanding that God wanted us to be just like Jesus and that we can do even greater works than He can do...that's powerful! I mean, we can heal, we can speak healing and prosperity to other people.

It just gives you a whole new dimension in what it means to know Christ. I mean it's better. It's not that you just accept Christ and you go to Heaven. That's great, but you miss too much. Right now, we walk in power! It's the realization that we can actually walk in the miracles of God, right now, today. We can have what we desire right now. We don't have to wait until we get to Heaven. We are healed right now. We have the power of Christ right now.

I am so excited and thank you Joseph for taking the lead on this important teaching. I just hope that this revelation would be spread to more believers and unbelievers so that they'll know the power that we have. Because we walk like Jesus walked because He lives in us."

It is all about getting it ingrained in your mind, in your heart that you are righteous and pure. That you are as powerful as Jesus is right now today.

It's all about you being able to believe that, I mean truly believe it in your heart, regardless of what your surrounding circumstances look like right now.

It is about being able to look past what the world calls facts and believing what God said.

It is about changing your thought pattern from one of a consciousness of sin, to the consciousness of righteousness and then keeping your mind there.

If the thought occurred to you that it might take a little practice changing your mind like that, you are right. And I have a very simple method that will help you set your mind firmly on the right track to develop a consciousness of righteousness.

All you need to do is become aware.

Key Consciousness Points - Chapter 3
Adam and Eve:
The Origin of Sin Consciousness

1. Adam and Eve were born in the perfect image of God Himself. They were born pure, holy and the righteousness of God.

2. Adam and Eve sinned and severed their perfect relationship with God, which caused them to live in a state of sin and the consciousness of sin.

3. They then passed along that state of sin and consciousness to all of their descendants. Hence, when we are born, we are born into sin and have a consciousness of sin.

4. When Jesus sacrificed and died on the cross, He took our sin and gave us His righteous, restoring righteousness to everyone who is born again.

5. When we are saved, we are born with a new, regenerated spirit. We are born again with the same pure and holy spirit that Adam had and we are born the righteousness of God.

Impartation Prayer

Dear Lord,

I thank You because in the beginning, everything you created was very good including our human race. Since that time Your mind and Your love for us never changed, in spite of Adam and Eve's disobedience. Instead, You took on human form Yourself, lowered Yourself to come down and restore the human race back to our original state, the consciousness of righteousness again.

Now Father I just love You, adore You and worship You for the righteous blood that was shed for me on the cross.

That's how I become righteous before You. Now I agree to receive everything that comes with my righteousness.

Glory to my Lord and Savior! Amen!

CHAPTER 4

Developing a Consciousness of Righteousness

Yes, we are born, or actually, we are born *again*, the righteousness of God. Jesus has restored righteousness. Righteousness is what we are. There is no need to gain it, or earn it or learn it. We *are* it! Amen.

You might say, "Okay, Joseph. That sounds wonderful. But if we are it, if we are already righteousness, how come we have such a hard time living it? How come it is so difficult for us to adapt to a consciousness of righteousness?"

Those are good questions. I mean, if we regain the total righteousness of God at the moment we get saved and are reborn, then why do we not instantly have a consciousness of righteousness? How come we continue with a mind that is focused on sin?

Wow! Now we are getting to the crux of what this book is all about. Let's take a look at these issues.

Obstacles to a Consciousness of Righteousness

There are some major obstacles and hindrances to you automatically or naturally turning to righteousness thinking when you are born again. True, at the moment of rebirth, at the moment of salvation, you are instantly the righteousness of God. However, several obstacles stand in the way of your thinking; of the way your mind works.

These things prevent you from immediately being able to *accept* and *receive* what you are. They hamper your perception and make it harder for you to become aware of what you are and what you have and to truly believe it in your heart.

Body, Mind (or Soul) and Spirit

You have to remember that at salvation; only one part of you is born again. You are made of three

78

parts; that is you are made in a *triune* nature, just like God. In this way we are made in His image.

You know of the Holy Trinity in that, God is One God, who manifests Himself in three persons.

God the Father
God the Son
God the Holy Spirit

God the Father is essentially the Godhead, the leader, the Almighty Creator.

God the Son is the body, the flesh. God the Son is God in human form; of course that being Jesus the Christ.

God the Holy Spirit is the nature, the essence, the spirit of God.

When God said, "Let us make man in *our* image, He meant in the image of His three persons; that's Who He was talking to; Himself, or selves. Therefore we are:

Mind(Soul)
Body
Spirit

The mind is the soul, the main consciousness, the leader.

The body is our body, our flesh.

The spirit is our nature and the true essence, the true spirit of God, what we are.

In a diagram, it might look like this...

† The Father = the head, lead conscious

† The Son = the body, flesh

† The Spirit = the spirit, essence, nature

We are made up as:

• Soul/Mind = the head, lead conscious, soul

• Body = the body, flesh

• Spirit = the spirit, essence nature

In God's Image

The Father
Head

God

The Son
Flesh

Holy Spirit
Nature

Body
Flesh

Spirit
Nature

Man

Mind
Head/Soul

Essentially, you are a spirit. First and foremost, you are a spirit. You are a spirit that is housed or incased in a body; a body made from the dust of the earth. That body is directed by a living soul; a mind or consciousness.

At salvation, only one part of your three parts is actually born again and that is your spirit. Remember?

"And if Christ be in you, the body is dead because of sin; but the Spirit is life because of righteousness."

---Romans 8:10(KJV)

The body, the flesh is dead, but if Christ be in you, you have a *new spirit*, that is life! The spirit is life, why? Because of the righteousness of God.

Your body, your flesh as well as your brain remain the same, as the Holy Spirit creates a new spirit.

Your body and your brain remain the same, including all of their old habits and ways. You may have noticed that if you could not jump up and slam-dunk a basketball before you got saved; after you got saved, you still could not dunk.

If you could not remember and recite the Gettysburg Address or perform complex geometric statistical analysis in your mind before you got saved; you still could not do such things after you got saved.

Your body and mind stay the same. This is why you have to *retrain* your mind and body to adapt to your new spirit.

"I beseech you therefore, brethren, by the mercies of God, that ye present your bodies a living sacrifice, holy, acceptable unto God, which is your reasonable service.
And be not conformed to this world: but be ye transformed by the renewing of your mind, that ye may prove what is that good, and acceptable, and perfect, will of God."
---Romans 12:1-2(KJV)

The Lord told us in His Word, very simply, what we need to do. He said sacrifice your body, keep it Holy, clean, and renew your mind

Your body and mind do not simply or automatically switch over and begin to follow your new spirit. You have to do something to lead your body and your mind. You have to allow your spirit to take the lead.

I will put it as plain as I can. Developing a consciousness of righteousness does not happen by itself. You have to *make it happen*. It is a deliberate and conscious act on your part. It is a deliberate and intentional act, an act of faith.

The World, the Flesh and the Devil

So, first there is your very own body, your flesh and your own mind that hinders you from coming into the full consciousness of your God given righteousness. In addition to that, the enemy and the ways of this world have something to do with it as well.

The devil knows the power you will gain once you come into the realization of your righteousness nature, and it is the last thing he wants to happen. So, he does what any reasonably capable enemy would do; he tries to prevent you for getting there in the first place.

So, first the consciousness of righteousness is so simple and plain that most of us miss it. Then, our flesh and minds have a difficult time changing to adapt to our new spirit and our new nature.

Finally, the devil, using lies, deceit, trickery, the world and worldly things, is doing everything he can to stop us from seeing and becoming aware of our righteousness standing. You can have all the righteousness you want, but if you are not aware of it, it makes no difference.

Remember our story with the man on the boat. He had every possible comfort and everything he could ever want to eat, yet since he was unware of this; he suffered and nearly starved to death.

With such opposition, I think you can forgive yourself for not already getting it. But we can do better than that. Let's do more; let's take action right now.

I have developed a plan, a simple step-by-step plan that will help you move into the consciousness of righteousness and help you stay there. It is a simple plan, though it may not always be that easy. All you need to do is remember the word, Aware.

Consciousness is awareness and we need to become consciousness or *aware* of our righteousness. So concentrate on the word, the acronym aware.

A.W.A.R.E.

Keep this acronym in mind to get and stay in a consciousness of righteousness. First, I will briefly go over each letter of the acronym, and then we will get deep into each.

A = Awake
W = Walk
A = Accept
R = Receive
E = Eternal

A = Awake

Yes, that is exactly what it sounds like. The first thing you need to do is wake up! *Wake up and smell the coffee*, as they say. You need to wake up and realize. Wake up and know. Wake up to the knowledge.

There is an ancient Chinese Proverb that goes:

He who does not know and does not know that he does not know, is a fool, shun him.
He who does not know and knows that he does not know, is a child, teach him.
He who knows and does not know that he knows, is asleep, awake him.
But he who knows and knows that he knows, is wise, follow him.

At this point, you know and you do not yet *know* that you know; hence you are asleep and you need to wake up! Then, you will know and you will know that you know!

The first A in A.W.A.R.E. stands for awake and by the time we finish that chapter, I promise that you will be awake having the full *knowledge* of righteousness and of what you know, and you will know that you know.

W = Walk

Once you have the knowledge, then you need to begin to walk by faith. We need to walk in Christ. I know we all love to quote the old saying, "We walk by faith, not by sight."

Well, that is really not accurate. Most of us, usually walk purely by sight; that is, we make decisions normally based on what we see and what our five senses tell us.

I think that is because most of us confuse *faith* with simply believing. We think that to have faith is some sort of psychological or even meta-physical thing. We equate faith with state of mind.

The truth is that faith is essentially a verb; it is an action word. Faith is something you do; you *exercise* faith.

You say you have faith that the hammock hanging way up there on the top of that tree will hold your weight. Okay, but that is not faith.

Faith is to climb up there and jump in the hammock! If you believe the hammock will hold you, then go ahead and get in it. That is faith.

Once you have the knowledge of righteousness, which you will by the end of Chapter 5 = A, then you will learn to walk in faith, to exercise your faith and to walk in Him!

As ye have therefore received Christ Jesus the Lord,
so walk ye in him:
Rooted and built up in him, and stablished in the faith, as ye
have been taught, abounding therein with thanksgiving.

Beware lest any man spoil you through philosophy and vain
deceit, after the tradition of men, after the rudiments of the
world, and not after Christ.

For in him dwelleth all the fulness of the Godhead bodily.
And ye are complete in him, which is the head of all
principality and power:

In whom also ye are circumcised with the circumcision made
without hands, in putting off the body of the sins of the flesh
by the circumcision of Christ:

---Colossians 2:6-11(KJV)

Good God! I want to keep going with this, but not yet. We will get into it in Chapter 6 = W.

A = Accept

After you have gained the knowledge of righteousness and then you begin to walk in Him, to walk in righteousness, you will need to accept God's way.

What I mean is that as you go and grow in your walk, you are going to run into some strong opposition to your walk. That opposition is going to challenge you and everything that you believe. That strong opposition is going to come mostly from you.

Your flesh and your mind, aided and influenced by the devil, is going rise up and challenge you on many occasions.

You say, "Wait a minute! I thought I was past all of that. I thought I was now as righteousness as Adam and Eve were!"

You are. However, this taunting and challenging does not stop. Plus, you have to remember, your mind and body have a lot more experience listening and following the ways of the world than they do following your new spirit.

How old were you when you got saved? Let us say that you were 23 years old when you received salvation. Okay, then your body and mind had 23 years of practice and experience in doing things by the ways of the world; 23 years following your sinful nature. Now, consider how long you have been saved; five years, seven years? You get the idea?

Does that mean that you will not be able to enjoy the full spectrum of a consciousness of righteousness until you have been saved as many years as unsaved?

Oh, no, no, no! You will have and walk in the full state and full consciousness of righteousness by the time you finish this book or before. However, you always have to keep one eye open.

Yes, you will have the consciousness of righteousness of Adam and Eve and still there will come opposition to Gods' way. What you will have to do is stand strong, stand firm and do not sway in the ways of the Lord. You will need to stand strong even when all of your senses tell you different.

You, with the devil's influence, will challenge God's way and make it look like it is the right way. Even with the consciousness of righteousness of Adam and Eve, this can happen. Remember this...

"And the serpent said unto the woman, Ye shall not surely die..."

---Genesis 3:4(KJV)

Here is Eve, spiritually pure, the pure and perfect righteousness of God. She gets into a conversation with the enemy and clearly tells him what God said, she tells him Gods' way.

"And the woman said unto the serpent, We may eat of the fruit of the trees of the garden:

But of the fruit of the tree which is in the midst of the garden, God hath said, Ye shall not eat of it, neither shall ye touch it, lest ye die."

Then came the voice of opposition. The voice wasn't harsh, mean and hostile or threatening. No, No. The voice was calm, cool and reasonable. The voice echoed *her* voice; it was what she was thinking.

And the serpent said unto the woman, Ye shall not surely die: For God doth know that in the day ye eat thereof, then your eyes shall be opened, and ye shall be as gods, knowing good and evil.

---Genesis 3:2-4(KJV)

That was it. That was all it took. The enemy came with something that looked right and sounded like it made sense, and that was all it took. You will be living the consciousness of righteousness, living a holier lifestyle and basking in the power of Jesus Christ Himself, and along will come the voice of the enemy.

When, and I emphasize *when*, this happens to you, you will need to stand strong and accept and submit to God's way. I give you a few ways to help you stay on track in the chapter on the first A = Accept.

R = Receive

The R in A.W.A.R.E. stands for receive, in that you need to totally receive the consciousness of righteousness.

Remember I said that you cannot learn or get or earn the consciousness of righteousness. You may learn all *about* it and understand it, but you will still have to completely receive it.

When you receive it, it becomes you and you become it. When you truly receive it, it becomes part of your heart. It becomes who and what you are.

For instance, you can accept a gift and not receive it. You can accept and understand a gift or a benefit and not receive it.

This takes a minute fully to explain, but by the end of Chapter 8 = R, you will have fully received the righteousness of God.

E = Eternal

I can only tell you this; if by the end of this chapter on the E = Eternal, if you are not jumping, screaming and running around shouting glory to God, then you might want to have someone check your pulse!

I don't want to give too much away in this brief introduction, so all I will say is I am sure you have heard the old saying that you are a *sinner saved by grace,* right?

We have all heard that, and are used to saying it so much that most people largely regard it as scripture.

"I am just a sinner, saved by the grace of God."

Well let me tell you this; by the end of chapter E = Eternal, not only will you know for a fact that the above statement is not scriptural, but you will know and understand exactly why is it is not even true.

You are *not* a sinner saved by grace. Not only that; you are not a sinner saved by grace and *you never were!* What?

Am I saying that you were never a sinner saved by grace?

No. I am saying that...

You were never a sinner, period!!!

Oh my God! Good gracious man! By the time you finish that chapter, you will really, really get it!

You are righteousness and as pure as the living Christ! Let's get to it!

Key Consciousness Points - Chapter 4
Developing a Consciousness of Righteousness

1. Though you can fully have a genuine consciousness of righteousness, your body and soul do not automatically or naturally adapt to this new way of your spirit.

2. At salvation, only one part of you is born again and new, and that is your spirit. Your body and soul remain the same and must be retrained.

3. The world, the flesh and the devil constantly converge to try to block you from ever becoming aware of your righteousness standing that is in your spirit and your heart.

4. Developing a consciousness of righteousness requires a deliberate and intentional act on your part, an act of faith.

5. A simple plan to remember is A.W.A.R.E. A = Awake, W = Walk, A = Accept, R = Receive, E = Eternal.

Impartation Prayer

Dear Father,

I thank You very much for making me aware of my righteousness! Now I know it is an intentional act on my part, an act of faith for me to receive it.

Right here, right now and forever I believe I am Your righteousness as Jesus is and I embrace it in my life as the ultimate truth.

I agree to have Your righteousness activated in my mind and my body as it already done in my Spirit.

Thank You Father, it is so! Amen!

CHAPTER 5

A = Awake

Yes, the very first thing you need to do in establishing a consciousness of righteousness and maintain it is to wake up to the fact that you already *are* it. You need to shift your focus from you to it. Let me explain.

Actually, righteousness, salvation, holiness and such are not about you. Your salvation is not and was never all about you. None of it is really about you, aside from the fact that God loves you so much. However, none of it is about anything that you do, did,

did not do or ever could do. All of it is about Him. It has to do with the first Adam and the second Adam.

The first Adam is of course the first man on earth. The person often referred to as the second Adam, is Jesus Christ. It is not about you. It is all about Christ.

The Bible explains it clearly in the Fifth chapter of Romans. For your convenience, here it is in the King James Version. Check it out and then we will break it down.

"Therefore being justified by faith, we have peace with God through our Lord Jesus Christ:
2 By whom also we have access by faith into this grace wherein we stand, and rejoice in hope of the glory of God.
3 And not only so, but we glory in tribulations also: knowing that tribulation worketh patience;

4 And patience, experience; and experience, hope:
5 And hope maketh not ashamed; because the love of God is shed abroad in our hearts by the Holy Ghost which is given unto us.

6 For when we were yet without strength, in due time Christ died for the ungodly.

⁷ For scarcely for a righteous man will one die:

yet peradventure

for a good man some would even dare to die.

⁸ But God commendeth his love toward us, in that,

while we were yet sinners, Christ died for us.

⁹ Much more then, being now justified by his blood, we

shall be saved from wrath through him.

¹⁰ For if, when we were enemies, we were reconciled to God by

the death of his Son, much more, being reconciled,

we shall be saved by his life.

¹¹ And not only so, but we also joy in God through our Lord

Jesus Christ, by whom we have now received the atonement.

¹² Wherefore, as by one man sin entered into the world, and

death by sin; and so death passed upon all men,

for that all have sinned:

¹³ (For until the law sin was in the world: but sin is

not imputed when there is no law.

¹⁴ Nevertheless death reigned from Adam to Moses, even over

them that had not sinned after the similitude of Adam's

transgression, who is the figure of him that was to come.

¹⁵ But not as the offence, so also is the free gift. For if through the offence of one many be dead, much more the grace of God, and the gift by grace, which is by one man, Jesus Christ, hath abounded unto many.

¹⁶ And not as it was by one that sinned, so is the gift: for the judgment was by one to condemnation, but the free gift is of many offences unto justification.

¹⁷ For if by one man's offence death reigned by one; much more they which receive abundance of grace and of the gift of righteousness shall reign in life by one, Jesus Christ.) ¹⁸ Therefore as by the offence of one judgment came upon all men to condemnation; even so by the righteousness of one the free gift came upon all men unto justification of life.

¹⁹ For as by one man's disobedience many were made sinners, so by the obedience of one shall many be made righteous. ²⁰ Moreover the law entered, that the offence might abound. But where sin abounded, grace did much more abound: ²¹ That as sin hath reigned unto death, even so might grace reign through righteousness unto eternal life by Jesus Christ our Lord."

---Romans 5:1-21(KJV)

Even your salvation is not about what you did or did not do, it is all about what He did over two thousand years ago.

In waking up, I mean that you need to get your mind off yourself and more on Him and what He did *for* you. You need to stop seeking self-righteousness and seek Him. Seek first, His kingdom and righteousness and everything else will be added.

"But seek ye first the kingdom of God, and his righteousness; and all these things shall be added unto you."
---Matthew 6:33(KJV)

If you keep your mind trained on Christ, you will have perfect peace.

"Thou wilt keep him in perfect peace, whose mind is stayed on thee: because he trusteth in thee."
---Isaiah 26:3(KJV)

You need to stop thinking about you. You need to get out of your mind what you did last week, or what you said last night. Stop thinking about what you thought and did not think and how you could have done something better.

That type of thinking is exactly what the enemy is looking for. The devil is the one who constantly accuses you. He is the accuser of the brethren.

"And I heard a loud voice saying in heaven, Now is come salvation, and strength, and the kingdom of our God, and the power of his Christ: for the accuser of our brethren is cast down, which accused them before our God day and night."
---Revelation 12:10(KJV)

It is not about you. Righteousness as well as unrighteousness are not made or controlled by human behaviors and that includes yours. It is not about us.

When we are born, we are born into sin. Period. Adam and Eve ensured that. We are born into sin and that is it. There was nothing that we could have done to change or prevent that. That was our condition at birth. It is a matter of our spiritual condition and personally, we could do nothing to fix it.

It did not matter how good you were or how moral you acted. It did not matter how much you read the Bible or how often you went to church or how much money you donated to the local charity. There was simply no behavior that you could have adapted that would make you saved.

To obtain salvation, you had to wake up and realize that it was not about you. You had to wake up and realize that you had to rely on and accept the gift of Christ. That was it.

The same holds true for salvation and righteousness. When you are born again, this time into the righteousness of God, there is nothing that you are going to do to change that.

You can't make a mistake, mess up or say the wrong thing and suddenly you are no longer the righteousness of God. No, no.

You are the righteousness of God, period. Your spirit is pure and holy and your spirit cannot sin. Your spirit is holy. Let me repeat that, as it bears repeating; you have to get this:

**Your new spirit is directly connected to God
and cannot sin. Your spirit is holy.**

If you have trouble believing me, please believe His Word…

"Whosoever is born of God doth not commit sin; for his seed remaineth in him: and he cannot sin, because he is born of God."

---1 John 3:9(KJV)

Your behavior, or should I say the behavior of your physical parts; your body and mind, cannot cancel your righteousness standing with God. What Christ did ensures this. Christ guaranteed that when He comes back, you would be counted free from all sin and guilt. The Lord told us that you will be held blameless.

"Who shall also confirm you unto the end, that ye may be blameless in the day of our Lord Jesus Christ."

---1 Corinthians 1:8(KJV)

Okay. Some may ask, "Does your behaviour have anything to do with it?" And the answer is yes; in particularly concerning the quality of life you have here on earth. However, you also have to remember that now you have a new spirit, a new nature; a new essence of what you are. Your heart is no longer the same. Now who you are, the very essence of you, is now like Christ.

So, your body and your mind may screw it up, do the wrong thing and even sin, but it cannot penetrate your spirit. You remain the righteousness of God! Your spirit is sealed.

When God purchased you with the price of His one and only begotten Son, the innocent and pure blood of Jesus; the Holy Spirit *sealed* your spirit.

This only makes sense. I mean think about it. Would God go through all of this trouble; sacrificing His Son, trading His righteousness for our sin and saving all of humankind, only so that the devil could come along a little later and reverse the whole thing?

Would God go through all of that trouble and effort to save you, just to watch you make a simple mistake, which He already knows you will make, and watch you nullify everything He did? Of course God would take measures to ensure that this glorious work was permanent, wouldn't you?

The moment you got saved, the minute you believed and accepted the gift of Christ, the Holy Spirit stepped in and *sealed the deal*!

"In whom ye also trusted, after that ye heard the word of truth, the gospel of your salvation: in whom also after that ye believed, ye were sealed with that holy Spirit of promise,

Which is the earnest of our inheritance until the redemption
of the purchased possession, unto the praise of his glory."
                                              ---Ephesians 1:13-14(KJV)

You have been bought, purchased and sealed,
clearing the path for your Heavenly reunion.

"But the path of the just is as the shining light, that shineth
more and more unto the perfect day."
                                              ---Proverbs 4:18(KJV)

Allow me to summarize the entire process, the
full path of what happened. Let me take a minute to
briefly summarize the history of, well...*everything*.

Creation and the Fall

God created the world, the spirit of humankind
and then made Adam and Eve, all free from sin.
Humans were directly *connected* to God; we had sort of
a holy umbilical cord. Then Adam sinned and severed
humankind's holy umbilical cord to God and they were
separated from God in that way. Sin then, made its entry
into the world through that one man, Adam. Through
sin came sickness, death and everything else.

Adam and Eve's condition, being separated from God, was passed on to all of their offspring, the entire human race. Thus, everyone born is born into a state of sin. Everyone is born in the condition of sin and possessing a sinful nature.

This is a condition and you cannot change it by your behavior or anything else. It is a condition of our existence. This condition would remain in place until someone or something paid for the sin. Someone had to atone for the sin of all humankind. This someone, of course, had to be pure and without sin.

Since every human was in sin from the moment of his or her birth, and no human could live a life within the laws that God gave humankind, no human could atone for the sin of humankind.

The Good News

God then had to, or should I say, *chose* to, save us. God would have to come to earth, be born without sin and live a life according to the law, His law; those 613 commandments. Then He would have to sacrifice Himself, the only perfect person on earth, and die for the repayment of our sins.

However, this posed some immediate challenges. God, the Father, in the person of the

Almighty Creator, could not come to earth. It's like light and darkness trying to occupy the same space at the same time. Good heavens! His pureness would annihilate a sinful world.

Ah, but remember the three persons of God!

† God the Father – the head of the Godhead
† God the Son – The flesh, the body, Jesus
† God the Holy Spirit – The essence and nature

Remember, God existed in this form before everything. Do you think maybe He knew what was going to happen and what He was going to do?

God the Father could not come to earth. God the Holy Spirit would not be appropriate for this situation as humankind was not yet ready and to able accept a new nature at this point. However, God the Son was perfect.

Now, God would have to be born on earth. He would have to be *born* or He could not be human, right? God would then choose a human woman to be born unto. He would choose a woman who was a virgin.

The reason for this is simply that if the woman had intercourse with a human man, then her womb and internal organs would no longer be pure but defiled by sinful man. Thus, if the Son were to be born through that vessel, He too would be born in sin. God needed a human woman who was good and still a virgin.

God would *spiritually* plant His seed into this woman. The resulting birth would be a baby whose mother was human and whose Father was God.

Hence, a baby born like this would be human flesh on the outside and God on the inside. This child would be God, fully God on the inside, wrapped in the human flesh of a man; that is to say, God *incarnate*. Of course, that is Jesus.

This would also result in the child Jesus, since He is not a direct descendant of Adam and Eve, He would not be born into sin.

It startles me how some theologians and clergy today still question and some simply do not believe in the virgin birth. However, if you think about it, a virgin birth is the only way it *could* have happened. It was the only way Jesus could be born on earth in a sin-free condition.

Anyway, Jesus would come, live a sinless life, thus becoming the only human qualified to be the sacrifice for humankind, or the *Lamb of God*. He would then sacrifice Himself on the cross at Calvary and absorb all of our sin while exchanging that sin and unrighteousness with His pure and holy righteousness. He would become our savior, the Christ.

So, by one man, Adam, sin came into the world; by one man Jesus, the grace of God covered all sin. With the sacrificial death of Jesus, the sin problem was forever solved, it is over, that is it; it is done. No matter what, God's grace will always overcome sin.

"Moreover the law entered that the offense might abound. But where sin abounded, grace abounded much more, so that as sin reigned in death, even so grace might reign through righteousness to eternal life through Jesus Christ our Lord."
---Romans 5:20-21(KJV)

Thus, once you accept what Jesus Christ did for you on the cross, that's it. Case closed. Sin is dead in your life and you are the righteousness of God, period. You were a slave to sin, when you had a sinful nature, but no more!

In fact, the more you concentrate on sin and your behavior, the more you nullify the work and the sacrifice of our Lord and savior. Heaven forbid!

I'll give you one last thing that may help you grasp this. Let's look at it from another angle. Let's go back to Genesis and take a quick look at the story of creation.

Remember from your Sunday School days, that God created everything in six days. He did all of His work and created everything that was ever created in six days, and then on the seventh day He rested. After that sixth day, nothing new was ever created. Everything that came after those six days, He made from the elements that He already created *during* those six days.

Cars, flat-screen televisions, computers, cell phones, every new luxury and high-tech device that there is and ever will be, were all created over two thousand years ago. That is, all of the *elements* to make those things, God created during those six days. Today, all we do is take things that were already here from the beginning of time, and combine them in ways that *construct* new things. But they were all created during the six days of creation. That is why the Bible says that there is really nothing new under the sun.

> *"The thing that hath been, it is that which shall be;*
> *and that which is done is that which shall be done:*
> *and there is no new thing under the sun."*
>
> ---Ecclesiastes 1:9(KJV)

This is also why God is the one and only true Creator. To create, in the true sense of the word, is to make something from nothing. Only God can do that.

So, let's continue to play this out.

> *"So God created man in his own image, in the image of God*
> *created he him; male and female created he them."*
>
> ---Genesis 1:27(KJV)

God creates humans in His image. He created them both at the same time, male and female. Then God goes on and gives them some instructions on what they are to do; be fruitful and multiply and all those good things.

> *"And God blessed them, and God said unto them, Be fruitful,*
> *and multiply, and replenish the earth, and subdue it: and*

have dominion over the fish of the sea, and over the fowl of the air, and over every living thing that moveth upon the earth."

---Genesis 1:28(KJV)

God gave them a few more instructions and finally...

"And God saw every thing that he had made, and, behold, it was very good. And the evening and the morning were the sixth day."

---Genesis 1:31(KJV)

There are two things that I want you to see in this last verse of the first chapter of Genesis. The first thing is that at the end of every day of creation, God looked back over His work and He said it was good.

But when He created us, He said it was *very good!* Good God! The Almighty Creator creates the whole world, the universe in fact; billions of stars, the sun and the moon and He said all of that stuff was *just good.*

Then He created us and we were *better* than good! Goodness; that is enough to celebrate who you are right there!

The second thing to note is that this was the end of the six days. That's it. God is done creating things. After this, He rested. God did not create one single thing after this point. Here is the question:

Where are Adam and Eve?

Feel free to go ahead and get into your Bible right now and look. But there is no mention of Adam and Eve during the six days of creation.

You might say that the male and female that God created and was talking to were Adam and Eve. But if that is true, then how can you explain what happens later in Genesis?

"And the Lord God formed man of the dust of the ground,
and breathed into his nostrils the breath of life;
and man became a living soul."

---Genesis 2:7(KJV)

Here in the second chapter of Genesis, well after God had finished all His work, rested and then blessed and sanctified the seventh day, then here comes Adam.

How do you reconcile this? Here is what happened.

In the six days, God *created the spirit* of man and woman. He created the spirit of humankind. Remember, we are made of three parts:

1. Mind (Soul)
2. Body
3. Spirit

During the six days of creation, God created only the spirit part. He created only the perfect and holy part of us. That's all. This is how we can see where the Holy part of us comes from. This is a definitive breakdown of the three parts of what we are. That is the essence of what we are. That is the essence of what you are. The foundation of what you are is a spirit. That is the only part of you that God *created*. Again, you are first a spirit.

Later, God *forms*; that is He shaped or molded the body of man from the dust, the dirt. This dust was already here, created during those six days.

This is also a clear indication of the nature of your body. Your body is of this earth. Your body is not holy or connected to God. Only your spirit is. Now, here is the main thing I want you to see on this point.

After God forms the body, then He *breathed the breath of life* into that mound of dirt and it became alive, aware, and conscious. Are you with me? You can clearly see the three parts of what we are.

What God had when this was all over was a spirit (one part) that He put inside of a body (second part), and then He gave that body an awareness, a consciousness or a mind, that many people refer to as the "soul" (third part). That mind or soul is also not holy; it is merely the driving force or the director of the dirt made body.

If I had to illustrate what we are, it might look a little something like this:

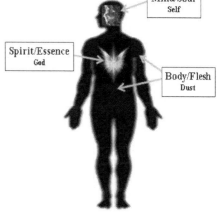

So, there is Adam, and then God creates Eve from his rib, or his womb (hence *womb*-man or woman) and thus, they both have the make up as depicted.

However, I want you to look at where and how the soul comes into the picture. God breathed the breath of life, into this lifeless mound of dirt, and it became alive.

In a way, it reminds me of the childhood fantasy tale of "Frosty the Snowman." You remember the story and the song by Gene Autry of the snowman built by a couple of kids. They made him and then they began putting on the different parts of the snowman, like a carrot for his nose and pieces of coal for his eyes. However, when they added on this magical hat, Frosty came to life; he just woke up!

First, he is just a few big balls of snow and the moment the hat hits his head, he wakes up, and was a conscious soul. This is the situation with Adam. God breaths into the dirt and he wakes up; he gains consciousness, an awareness.

God had created the spirit earlier, and then He made a body from the dust and breathed life into that body which woke it up.

The reason I get into this is because this is the same situation you have right now. In fact, as you get deeper into Biblical culture, you find that most things in life repeat themselves. They happen over and over. I get deep into examples of this in my next book on the meaning of being born again.

Anyway, so God gave you a new spirit at salvation, but you still have your same old body and mind. Now you need to take in the breath of God's righteousness and wake them up!

You need to accept the gift from God of His one and only begotten Son, and live your life like kings and queens.

Yes, we were once condemned, but we have been reconciled unto the Lord. Our account is clean and our debt is paid. We were once slaves to sin, but now we are free and pure in the eyes of God.

Yes, by one man death came to us all. But by one man, righteousness comes to us today. One man's disobedience made us all sinners. But by one man's perfect obedience, we can all be made righteous.

It is not about *you*!

The Lord Will Not Impute Sin

I think one of the best ways for you really to understand this so that you know it and know that you know it, is to explore the concept of imputation.

Just before that great explanation on the abolishment of sin in chapter five of Romans, the Lord talks about not imputing sin.

"Blessed is the man to whom the Lord will not impute sin."

---Romans 4:8(KJV)

To impute, in this reference, means to *charge to your account* or *to bill*, to *assess accountability*. As an example, you go into a restaurant and order a few things from the menu, perhaps an appetizer and some drinks.

The wait staff then *imputes* the costs of these items to your bill. They put or add the charges to your account for you eventually to pay and they hold you accountable for that payment.

You continue ordering and they continue imputing until you are ready to leave. At that time you have to settle the bill, somebody has to pay.

Now the restaurant may offer some forgiveness for some charges. As an example, they may offer some discount or wave some charges. In that case, they first impute the charge to your bill, and then they deduct it from the total. However, the charge is still imputed to the bill. Are you with me?

So, you go into the restaurant, order a bunch of things and as you are ready to pay the bill, they say, "Yes, your bill was $85, but now it is only $45, as we have discounted or *forgiven* some of the charges." Okay, that's great.

Now, what if someone were to pay your bill for you? What if someone, a total stranger, went up to the cashier before you checked out and fully paid your whole bill? In that case, it might sound like this,

"Yes, your bill was $85, but someone has paid it in full and you owe nothing."

Wow! Fantastic! That is grace, right? Actually, that scenario is similar to the thought of being a sinner saved by grace.

In other words, in the case above, it is clear that you had an outstanding bill; however, someone else paid it for you. Your bill was there, it was due, you did rack up the charges, but someone else paid the bill for you. That is beautiful.

However, what Jesus did for you and I is much more than any of the above examples.

You see, Jesus made it so the charges were never imputed to your account in the first place. Jesus made it so God blotted out the bill altogether!

"I, even I, am he that blotteth out thy transgressions for mine own sake, and will not remember thy sins."
---Isaiah 43:25(KJV)

Good God! The Lord did a lot more than simply give you a discount or forgive the bill. He got rid of the bill! God erased the bill. He has completely cleared the road for your redemption once and for all!

"I have blotted out, as a thick cloud, thy transgressions, and, as a cloud, thy sins: return unto me; for I have redeemed thee."

---Isaiah 44:22(KJV)

It's like going to check out of the restaurant and getting ready to pay your huge bill, and the waiter does not say that your bill has been paid, he says...

"What bill?"

You are the pure and holy righteousness of God! Wake up and accept it!

A Testimony

"What does it mean to me to be fully conscientious of my righteousness?

I know who I am. I finally understand all the scriptures I've been hearing nearly my whole life, and their amazing implications to my everyday life. I understand that I no longer have a sin nature because it was *traded* for a righteous nature at the cross.

Because of what Jesus did, I get true holiness and all the privileges of heaven that go with it. I am a new spirit creature created in God's image and fully equipped to walk as light on this earth.

Just thinking about who I am in Christ makes me stand a bit taller and walk with more dignity that is befitting a citizen of heaven! Best of all, I don't have to beg God for anything because it was and is His idea.

Knowing my righteousness refocuses me on my role as a co-laborer with Christ. I do not have to spend all my attention on hand to hand combat with the enemy just to keep him at bay and stay afloat. I have a new foundation of oneness with God that excites me to stay tuned in to the Holy Spirit and really move forward with my assignment on this earth.

Becoming truly conscious of my righteousness really is the first step to a Christian life. It is the 'real good news'."

Selena Herranen

Key Consciousness Points – Chapter 5
A = Awake

1. Neither righteousness as well as unrighteousness is about you. They are about Christ.

2. All sin came into the world by the disobedience of one man, Adam. Likewise, we can all gain righteousness by the obedience of one man, Jesus.

3. Your spirit, your new spirit, is holy, connected to God and cannot sin. Your body and mind can sin, but it cannot penetrate your spirit.

4. At salvation, you have the righteousness of God and there is nothing you can do to change that. There is no behavior that can change your righteous condition.

5. God did not and will not impute sin to those who are saved. Sin has never been charged to your account. You are not a sinner saved by grace. You are not a sinner…period!

Impartation Prayer

Dear Father,

I am so grateful today to finally know and understand that You have already paid my sin debt in full! By Your Holy Son Jesus, who died in my place for me to be free of sin. Thank you father!

From now on, sin I know you no longer have power and dominion over me because my Spirit is alive and sealed! I am free from sin and its power from now and forever! Amen! Alleluia! Alleluia! Alleluia! Alleluia! Alleluia! Give God glory!

CHAPTER 6

W = Walk

So, first wake up to the knowledge and understanding of who you are and what you are. You need first to become awake to the realization that none of this is about you. Shake the vanity and pride and understand that it is not about you.

This is all about Christ, Jesus. Everything is about Jesus...*everything*. In fact, that is the only valid question on earth. There is only one question on earth that anyone needs to answer and the way you answer it determines everything.

"Who is Jesus to you?" That's it. The way a person answers this determines everything. Who is Jesus to the world? I think you get my point.

Again, first get it into your head that it is not about you. Get it into your head that once you accepted the greatest gift of all gifts in time, the gift of salvation through our Lord and Saviour Jesus Christ, you became the righteousness of God.

Understand that once you are born again you have a new spirit and a new nature, the nature of Christ. Understand and believe that once born again, you are the righteousness of God. You are the righteousness of God, period. There is nothing that you can do to change it, stop it, reverse it or mess it up.

You cannot do anything about it, because it actually does not have a whole lot to do with you. It is about what Christ did on the cross. He bestowed that righteousness *on* you and then the Holy Spirit sealed the deal.

You didn't do anything to get it and you can't do anything to shake it. All you can do is accept it. You are the pure and holy righteousness of the one and only living God!

Now it is time to believe it and *walk* in it. It is time truly to begin to walk by faith. Unfortunately, to *walk by faith* has become such an overused term and a modern cliché that it has become much misunderstood.

It seems everyone and anyone is really quick to quote, that all too familiar line from 2 Corinthians,

> *"We walk by faith not by sight."*
>
> ---2 Corinthians 5:7(KJV)

You may even have said this and believe that you do walk by faith, and I pray you do as well.

The truth, however, is that only a few people actually walk by faith and not by sight. Let us just look at a couple of very practical and common thoughts on the subject.

The Meaning of Faith

First, if we just take a closer look at what faith actually means, I think it becomes clear that we do not usually walk by faith. What is faith?

> *"Now faith is the substance of things hoped for,*
> *the evidence of things not seen."*
>
> ---Hebrews 11:1(KJV)

Of course, we first turn to the Bible's definition in Hebrews. Look at it in the Amplified Version below.

"Now faith is the assurance (title deed, confirmation) of things hoped for (divinely guaranteed), and the evidence of things not seen [the conviction of their reality—faith comprehends as fact what cannot be experienced by the physical senses]."

---Hebrews 11:1(AMP)

That is beautiful. The Bible tells us in Hebrews that faith is the *substance* of things hoped for. I like the way the Amplified version puts it, *the title deed, the confirmation.*

So, while I don't have the house or see the house, I have the title deed. I don't have the car, but I got the keys. I have something. I have something of substance that represents the thing that I hope for.

Further, faith is the conviction or the fact of something that I cannot prove by conviction or fact. Faith is the thing that makes me certain of the reality of something that my physical senses cannot detect.

So then, faith is my substantial belief in something that I am hoping for but cannot yet see, or something along those lines.

If you just think about it; that is the opposite of the way we all think. The way we think, in the natural that is, is the polar opposite of the idea of faith. As popular and common as the quote, *walk by faith* is, ever more common is this old axiom:

"Seeing is believing."

From birth, we know we are to believe that which we can see. *I won't believe until I see it! Show me! If I can't see it I don't believe it.*

What faith is saying is the exact opposite. Faith essentially says that *believing is seeing!* Believing is seeing and once you see it, only because you believed it, then it will become real.

What I mean is that normally we do not approach life in that way. We need some evidence, physical evidence before we believe in something.

Your belief in God and your belief that Jesus is real and alive are all by faith. There is no psychical evidence to any of it. Yet, you still believe it. Glory to God. However, such a belief would have to extend far past the belief in the resurrection of Jesus Christ. Your faith needs to extend to cover everything that God said in His Word.

So, while we may believe that we do things by faith, actually, that is not accurate.

You say you took that job purely on faith? I beg to differ. You already knew what the job was; you know people who do that sort of work. You knew it is legitimate work and you knew what the salary was going to be. Your decision may have had opposing choices, but your decision was not by faith.

People say that they have faith when they get on an airplane. It is faith because you don't know the condition of the pilot or the aircraft so you have to just have faith in the whole thing.

I am sorry to tell you but this too is not faith. You know of airplanes, you know what they are. You may have flown before or know someone who has flown before. Even if you have not flown on an airplane yourself, or do not know anyone who has, you know what airplanes are and basically how they work and you have seen them on television or live up in the sky.

You have *empirical physical evidence* that planes take off, fly and land safely. It is not having faith when you get on a plane. It may be having *trust*. You may trust the airline and the technology and trust in the overall odds of airline safety, but it is not faith.

To have faith is when faith, *itself* is the evidence. You have no other empirical evidence, history or data. You believe first, without any evidence, then and only then does the thing hoped for, come to be. You believe first, and then the thing materializes into substance on a physical level.

To walk by faith, therefore, is to walk and make decisions not only according to your faith and the things that you cannot see, but to do so in *contrast* to what your physical eyes see. To walk by faith is to make decisions, often life and death decisions, which are *contrary* to what your physical senses tell you are real.

Faith is to believe in God's Word and direction in spite of what you see as reality. Faith is to trust in the Lord and not to believe in what you see. Faith is to trust in the Lord in spite of what your own brain tells you.

"Trust in the Lord with all thine heart; and lean not unto thine own understanding."
---Proverbs 3:5(KJV)

The Bible tells us to trust in the Lord and not to lean to what we can actually understand. In fact, the Word says the person who believes in what he can see and understand is a fool!

"He that trusteth in his own heart is a fool:..."

---Proverbs 28:26a(KJV)

So, when you make that decision based on the fact that it looks good to you and that you understand everything about the situation, it is actually a foolish thing to do and is not operating in faith.

Here in lies the conundrum. We are all experts at taking what we think is best and convincing ourselves that it is God's way. We are very good at this, me included.

We make up our own minds, we decide what it is that we want and which way we want to go, then we convince ourselves that it is God's way and the direction of the Holy Spirit, and finally we pray and ask God to bless it.

Do you hear what I say?

Still think that you've been walking by faith? Look at it this way.

Exercising Faith

With the above explanations, it is easy to conclude that faith is all and only about believing, that it is all about a state of mind. Most people believe that faith is all about how you think and what you believe in your heart.

However, faith and walking by faith, living by faith is about much more than just a state of mind or a philosophical viewpoint.

Faith is actually about action; it is about doing something. Let's look at a few definitions of faith, starting with the basic, corporal definition from the dictionary.

Merriam-Webster

(1) belief and trust in and loyalty to God

(2) belief in the traditional doctrines of a religion

> b: firm belief in something for which there is no proof
>
> c: *clinging to the faith that her missing son would one day return*
>
> d: complete trust

Okay. That certainly sounds like faith. However, to understand truly the full meaning of the word, we have to go back to its origin. Let's go back to when the word first came to be.

The Hebrew Roots and Original Foundation of Faith

Let us just go straight to the meaning in the Hebrew where we see that the root word from which we get "faith", is "pistis." However, the verb is *pistueo.*

Faith, pistis, means belief, *firm persuasion,* assurance, firm conviction, faithfulness.

Belief or pistueo means to trust in and rely upon, commit to the charge of, confide in, have a *mental persuasion.*

It is the *act* whereby a person lays hold of God's resources, *becomes obedient to what He has prescribed* and putting aside all self-interest and self-reliance, trusts Him completely. It is an *unqualified surrender* of the whole of one's being in dependence upon Him. It is wholly trusting and relying upon Him for all things. It is <u>not just mental assent</u> to the facts and realities of truth; it must come from a deep inner conviction.

If we continue and go back to the Greek, we see that the Greek transliteration of the word faith is pistis.

"Strong's 4102: pistis

> (from 3982/*peithô*, "*persuade,* be persuaded") – properly, *persuasion* (be *persuaded,* come to trust); *faith*

> The root of 4102/*pistis* ("faith") is 3982/*peithô* ("to persuade, be persuaded") which supplies the *core-meaning* of faith ("*divine persuasion*"). It is God's warranty that guarantees the fulfillment of the revelation He births within the receptive believer (cf. 1 John 5:4 with Hebrews 11:1)."

Let me try to sum all of this up...

The main common denominator in the definition of faith, from Hebrew to Greek to current definition is *persuasion.* Faith is persuasion or act of being *fully persuaded.*

Merriam-Webster

Persuade: Transitive Verb

> (1) to move by argument, entreaty, or expostulation to a belief, position, or course of action
> (2) to plead with: to urge

The point I am trying to make here is that you cannot have faith, true Godly faith, without persuasion. Faith is persuasion and persuasion is a verb.

In other words, there is no faith without the verb, without the action. There is no faith without action. Faith has to have action; that is, work must accompany the belief or faith is void. This is why faith without works is dead.

"Even so faith, if it hath not works, is dead, being alone."
---James 2:17(KJV)

So you can have the faith, as far as the belief, but without an action it is worthless. If you say you have faith in that which you cannot see, then you must show it, demonstrate it by *doing*. You show your faith *by* your works.

Yea, a man may say, Thou hast faith, and I have works: shew me thy faith without thy works, and I will shew thee my faith by my works."
---James 2:18(KJV)

You say you have faith in my driving. Okay, then get in the car and let me drive you somewhere. To say you have faith in my driving, but when you see me get behind the wheel, you take off running; is proof that you *do not* have faith in my driving.

You say you have faith that you can get up and walk without a cane? Okay, then do it. If you notice, often when Jesus performed miracles, He had the person do that which they needed Him to do for them. He had them do something in faith, demonstrating faith and when they did it, the miracle took place. As an example, look at when Jesus healed the ten lepers.

*"And as he entered into a certain village, there met him ten
men that were lepers, which stood afar off:
And they lifted up their voices, and said, Jesus, Master,
have mercy on us.
And when he saw them, he said unto them, Go shew
yourselves unto the priests. And it came to pass,
that, as they went, they were cleansed."*
---Luke 17:12-14(KJV)

You have to understand the situation and the law concerning lepers at that time. Once you had this disease, you were banned from the city and from having any contact with the public.

So, here is Jesus and just as He enters this city He meets these ten men, who apparently were living on the very outskirts of the city, which makes sense. Even still, they stood *a far off.* If they approached Jesus or anyone who did not have the disease, they would be breaking the law.

So, they see Jesus and ask for help by shouting to Him from a distance.

"And they lifted up their voices, and said, Jesus, Master, have mercy on us."

But look at what Jesus tells them to do.

"And when he saw them, he said unto them, Go shew yourselves unto the priests."

What?! Are you kidding? They can't do that. They are not supposed to do that. In order to go show themselves to the priests, they would have to walk right through the middle of the town, and walk into some of the most holy and well-populated areas to locate the priests and approach them! It is very possible that such an act would have meant the death penalty for them, or they would have been stoned to death on the way.

Jesus did not say, "Go, and I will heal you has you go..." He made no mention of healing them at all. He just told them to go and that was it, and they started to go.

My God, that is faith in action! You would think one of them would have at least said, "Hey wait a minute! That's crazy! How are we going to do that?"

But no. There was no argument, not even a discussion; they just obeyed the Lord with pure, blind, childlike faith!

Please note that as they went, they were cleansed. Not before. They had to start; they had to *step out on faith*, before they realized and actualized the miracle. And that is exactly what you need to do now.

Walk by Faith

The W in A.W.A.R.E. stands for walk. Wherein now, after you have become awake and aware of what you are and what you have, in that you know now that you are the righteousness of God, no matter what; now you need to walk in that understanding. You need to begin to walk, being guided and directed by your spirit, rather than by your body and mind; rather than by what you see. You need to step out on your faith.

Now that you have got it, you have received Christ and the power, you need to walk and live in Him. You need to walk, being fully rooted and established in the faith, remembering that such faith is action.

"As ye have therefore received Christ Jesus the Lord,
so walk ye in him:
Rooted and built up in him, and stablished in the faith, as ye
have been taught, abounding therein with thanksgiving.

Beware lest any man spoil you through philosophy and vain
deceit, after the tradition of men, after the rudiments of the
world, and not after Christ.

For in him dwelleth all the fulness of the Godhead bodily.
And ye are complete in him, which is the head of all
principality and power:

In whom also ye are circumcised with the circumcision made
without hands, in putting off the body of the sins of the flesh
by the circumcision of Christ:"

---Colossians 2:6-11(KJV)

Good God! Is that not it? Breaking it down a little bit...

"As ye have therefore received Christ Jesus the Lord,
so walk ye in him: Rooted and built up in him,
and stablished in the faith..."

As I just said, now that you've got it, you are awake and you have accepted Him; walk in Him, live and exercise the faith.

"Beware lest any man spoil you through philosophy and vain
deceit, after the tradition of men, after the rudiments of the
world, and not after Christ."

Let me clarify, *"...lest any man spoil you through philosophy and vain deceit..."*does not mean what you may first think.

That word *spoil* in this context does not mean as in spoiled milk or something. Instead, think of it in the context of the *spoils of war*, the leftovers of a fight. The text is saying that you do not want to allow anyone to reduce you, use you and misdirect you to where you become nothing more than the leftovers of the conflict between God and evil. The way they could do this is through philosophy, or the thinking of man, that is our human thinking and vanity. This, by directing you to look at the things of the world, the things you can see and touch. It is the rudiments or the rewards that the world offers that all take you away from the persuasion of Christ.

"For in him dwelleth all the fulness of the Godhead bodily. And ye are complete in him, which is the head of all principality and power:"

In Him, (Christ, the Son, the body) is all the fullness of the Godhead. Jesus is fully God and remember the Godhead; the three Persons of God. Rely on Christ and you embrace the Godhead.

You are complete in Him! Complete in Him, which is the head, the leader the one in charge of all principality and power! Good Lord!

Right there, you should never again fear or even concern yourself with sin or the power of the enemy. Who and what is sin and the power of the enemy but...

"For we wrestle not against flesh and blood, but against principalities, against powers, against the rulers of the darkness of this world, against spiritual

wickedness in high places."

---Ephesians 6:12(KJV)

But who is in charge of all of the principality (or governing bodies) and powers and rulers of the darkness?

"And ye are complete in him, which is the <u>head of all</u> principality and power:"

My God, my God! Yes, He is the head of all principality and power. But hold on a minute. Once you embrace Him, once you walk in Him, and walk in the faith, being fully persuaded, and have fully received the righteousness of Him; then who wields the power of all principality? That's right...you!

"In whom also ye are circumcised with the circumcision made without hands, in putting off the body of the sins of the flesh by the circumcision of Christ:"

---Colossians 2:11(KJV)

Granted, this last verse in the text can be a bit confusing, especially in the King James. Check it out in the Amplified.

"In Him you were also circumcised with a circumcision not made with hands, but by the [spiritual] circumcision of Christ in the stripping off of the body of the flesh [the sinful carnal nature],"

---Colossians 2:11(AMP)

What this verse is essentially saying is that you have been circumcised; not by the psychical form of circumcision which was to show the cutting away of the foreskin that demonstrated the shedding of the old nature. But you have been *spiritually* circumcised; the old nature, the sinful nature has been cut away, the old spirit, has been stripped away and the clean and holy spirit remains. You are now pure. You have been circumcised by Christ!

You are the righteousness, the purity and power of the fullness of the Godhead! Glory be to God!

Is it starting to sink in yet? Let's continue.

Key Consciousness Points – Chapter 6
W = Walk

1. It is time for you to begin to walk by faith. You need to begin making decisions based more on your spirit rather than your flesh and what you see.

2. To walk by faith is the opposite of what we have always been taught. We need to change from the thought that *seeing is believing*, to the understanding that *believing is seeing*.

3. Faith is persuasion and persuasion is action. Faith requires action. Faith without action, without work, is dead.

4. When you walk by faith, you walk in Him; you walk in the righteousness of God.

5. As you walk in the fullness of what you are, the righteousness of God, you wield the power of the Godhead over all principalities and power!

Impartation Prayer

Dear Father,

I believe it is time for me to begin to walk by faith. From now on I will make decisions based more on my spirit which is one with Your Spirit, rather than my five senses.

I thank You for teaching me today that walking by faith is walking in the fullness of what I am and who I am, which is Your righteousness.

Now I wield the power of the Godhead over all principalities and power! What a wonderful Father You are and what an amazing person You made me to be. All the glory belongs to You, my sovereign Lord. Amen!

CHAPTER 7

A = Accept

Congratulations! You are on your way to developing a consciousness of righteousness. You are now awake and aware of who you are and what you are.

You have woken up to the reality, to the fact that you are righteous, period. You now realize that your righteousness actually does not have much to do with you; but it is all about Christ.

It is not about what you do, but what He has already done. It is not about how you perform, but how

He already performed. It is not about sin, it is about grace.

You have woken up!

Then you began to walk in the realization that you are pure and holy. You began to walk by the faith that you are not a sinner saved by grace, but that you are not a sinner at all...period.

You are beginning to walk in the direction of your new nature, your righteous nature.

You are beginning to put work behind the belief, as you know that faith is action.

You are starting to put action behind your belief. You are beginning to rely less and less on your own understanding and beginning to lean more on Him. Now you need to step just a bit further as we come to the next letter in A.W.A.K.E., the second A = Accept.

Very simply put, you need to accept God's way. You are beginning to lean less on your own understanding and you need fully to embrace this, as your own understanding and your mind are going to face some big challenges.

What I mean is that as you continue on your journey and growth, as you begin to walk in Him, you are going to face opposition. You are going to face some stiff opposition and mostly from an unlikely source.

That opposition is going to challenge you and everything that you believe. That strong opposition is going to come mostly from you.

Your flesh and your mind, those two parts of you that were not born again, will often stand in rebellion against you; against your new born-again spirit.

What?! You might think, "Wait a minute! I thought I was through with all of that. I thought that I had the fullness of the Godhead and was as pure and righteous as Adam and Eve.

Yes, you can wield the power of the Godhead and yes, you are as righteous as Adam and Eve.

Then, you might ask, why does your body and mind still keep messing with you?

It is because you still live in there! You still reside in the same old body and have the same old mind that you had before you got saved.

This is why it is so critical to make our bodies a living sacrifice and renew our minds by the Word of God.

"I beseech you therefore, brethren, by the mercies of God, that ye present your bodies a living sacrifice, holy, acceptable unto God, which is your reasonable service.

And be not conformed to this world: but be ye transformed by the renewing of your mind, that ye may prove what is that good, and acceptable, and perfect, will of God."

---Romans 12:1-2(KJV)

Of course, this takes time. However, renewing your mind and body to align with your new spirit, also takes some practice.

There are ways to greatly speed up the process and even to make it happen very quickly. First, of course, you need to stay constantly in the Word, and second you have to learn fully to accept it.

You have the gift and you have the power. You know who you are and what you are. You know that you are the righteousness of God and you are starting to take action in that faith.

However, you are still in control. Remember, God will not violate your free will. You will have to make decisions on an almost daily basis.

Yes, you are pure and the righteousness of God. However, that righteousness nature does not automatically take over and control you. You have to decide to allow your new nature to have its way, you have to allow your new spirit to reign supreme; you have to accept God's ways in everything you do.

If you thought that as soon as you developed the consciousness of righteousness that the battles would be over and that you would just walk in the divine light and your spirit would act like some sort of a force field, automatically repelling any evil that approached you; I am sorry to tell you that it is not quite like that. It is not automatic.

Now, in time, it will become *nearly* automatic. After a while, you will walk blindly and your actions and reactions will become nearly unconscious. However, getting to that point requires deliberate and intentional action and practice.

When situations arise that challenge your own thinking, you have to do what the Word says and truly lean not to your own understanding.

You will have to make the decision to accept God's way in spite of what you see, think or feel. You have to *choose* to act and in the manner of your renewed spirit.

"That ye put off concerning the former conversation the old man, which is corrupt according to the deceitful lusts; And be renewed in the spirit of your mind; And that ye put on the new man, which after God is created in righteousness and true holiness."

---Ephesians 4:22-24(KJV)

You have to choose to put off the former conversation; the old dialogue, actions and thought processes, and accept the righteousness and true holiness that has been created in you.

Let's take another look at Adam and Eve for a moment.

Yes indeed, you have the consciousness of righteousness and you are as pure as the first two humans in existence; Adam and Eve. However, remember what happened to them.

There they were, chilling out in the Garden of Eden; pure, righteous and immortal, and still came the opposition to Gods' way.

"And the serpent said unto the woman, Ye shall not surely die..."

---Genesis 3:4(KJV)

As we talked about earlier, here is Eve, spiritually pure, the pure and perfect righteousness of God. She gets into a conversation with the enemy and clearly tells him what God said, she tells him Gods' way.

"And the woman said unto the serpent, We may eat of the fruit of the trees of the garden:

But of the fruit of the tree which is in the midst of the garden, God hath said, Ye shall not eat of it, neither shall ye touch it, lest ye die."

Then came the voice of opposition. The voice wasn't harsh, mean, hostile or threatening. No. Remember, the voice was calm, cool and reasonable. The voice echoed *her* voice; it was what she was thinking.

And the serpent said unto the woman, Ye shall not surely die: For God doth know that in the day ye eat thereof, then your eyes shall be opened, and ye shall be as gods, knowing good and evil.

---Genesis 3:2-4(KJV)

That was it. That was all it took. The enemy came with something that looked right and sounded like it made sense to her, and that was all it took.

The point I want to make here is that at that moment, Eve had a conscious and deliberate decision that she had to make:

A. Choose to go with what looked good and felt right in her own mind

Or

B. Choose to accept God's way in spite of what she thought

We all know what she chose.

You will be living the consciousness of righteousness, living a holier lifestyle and basking in the power of Jesus Christ Himself, and along will come the sneaky, conniving voice of the enemy.

Fortunately, the devil still uses the same old tricks; in fact he uses the exact same old tricks. The enemy's challenges do not come at you in the form of opposition. The enemy's attack usually does not look like an attack or a bad or negative thing. Usually the attack of the enemy looks like something reasonable, sensible or even good. The attack may often come in the form of what looks like a blessing from God.

When, and I emphasize *when*, this happens you, will need to stand strong and accept and submit to what you know is God's way. You have to stand on His Word.

You will have to choose between what you see and what you know, and what God said; choose between what the facts show you and what the Lord God told you.

Even when you are walking fully in Christ, opposition forces that could result in potential calamites will arise. Take a look at this situation with the disciples of Jesus.

"And the same day, when the even was come, he saith unto them, Let us pass over unto the other side.
And when they had sent away the multitude, they took him even as he was in the ship. And there were also with him other little ships.

And there arose a great storm of wind, and the waves beat into the ship, so that it was now full.

And he was in the hinder part of the ship,
asleep on a pillow: and they awake him, and
say unto him, Master, carest thou not that we perish?

And he arose, and rebuked the wind, and said unto the sea,
Peace, be still. And the wind ceased,
and there was a great calm.

And he said unto them, Why are ye so fearful?
how is it that ye have no faith?

And they feared exceedingly, and said one to another,
What manner of man is this, that even
the wind and the sea obey him?

---Mark 4:35-41(KJV)

I am certain that you are familiar with this story or at least the last few verses of the text, and rightly so.

"Peace be still..." Good God almighty! That will make you want to shout every time. However, that is not the part of the chapter that I want to point out to you.

Rather, what I want you to notice is that here were some of the disciples in the boat with Jesus. That is, they are with Jesus in the flesh. Jesus, God incarnate, is right there with them and they know who He is. God is physically and tangibly right there in the boat with them.

The Lord God is in the boat and *then* the storm arose! My God, do you hear what I say?

When they began the journey, apparently the sea was calm. Then as they journeyed, with God Himself right there besides them, the storm arose. The storm arose, winds became fierce and waves flooded the boat. They are in the boat; it is filling up with water and being tossed to near capsizing…all while they are in the very presence of God. In fact, God is caught in the storm with them!

And there arose a great storm of wind, and the waves beat into the ship, so that it was now full.

The point I am making here is that as you develop the consciousness of righteousness and walk fully in Christ, the storms will still come!

What you have to do is, in spite of what it looks like to you, in spite of your life being tossed and turned, in spite of the fact that it looks like your entire world is about to capsize; you need to choose to accept the fact that God's way is the only way and lean to what He said no matter what.

Jesus is the way, the only way.

Jesus saith unto him, I am the way, the truth, and the life: no man cometh unto the Father, but by me.

---John 14:6(JKV)

Key Consciousness Points – Chapter 7
A = Accept

---

1. You must completely accept God's way in spite of everything else. You have to lean not to your own understanding.

2. You will face strong opposition from your own flesh; your mind and body aided by the enemy.

3. Your righteous nature will not take you over and control you; it is not automatic or subconscious.

4. You have to make a deliberate and intentional choice to accept and allow your new nature, your righteous nature to take control.

5. Even while you are walking fully in Christ and in righteousness, storms will still arise.

Impartation Prayer

Dear Lord,

I finally accept Your way completely in my life over everything else. I don't want to lean on my own understanding anymore.

At this present moment, I make a deliberate and intentional choice to accept and allow Your new nature, Your righteous nature to take control over my life.

I know it is so, because this is Your perfect will for me since the beginning of this world. Thank You Father and I love you! Amen!

CHAPTER 8
R = Receive

If you are already there, if you already arrived, if you have already shed sin consciousness and are living in the light of your righteousness nature, praise God!

If you are almost there, Amen! I am so excited for you as I remember when the revelation of the consciousness of righteousness hit me. Glory to God, what a day!

Let's take a quick look at the process to help you develop and maintain a consciousness of righteousness so far.

We explored the "A" in A.W.A.R.E. which stands for Awake. We know that the first thing to do is to wake up; to wake up your mind and your body to the truth that when born again, you became the very righteousness of God Himself.

We discovered that you do not have to work to become it, nor do you have to learn it or earn it; you simply must wake up to the fact that you already *are* it; the pure and holy righteousness of the one and only living God.

Then we looked at the W which means Walk, and we found that after we wake up to the realization, that we must then walk in it. That is, we must walk by faith which means to take action.

We need to begin to walk in the fullness of what we know we are. We need to understand that it is not about us, but all about the Lord Jesus Christ, and walk in Him; by faith and not by sight.

Then, in the last chapter we discussed the second A in the acronym which stands for Accept. In that chapter we found that we must fully accept God's way.

Your righteous nature will not hit you over the head and take over you or your actions. Righteousness will not control you or brainwash you into walking around all day long in some type of heavenly trance where you cannot do wrong or make a mistake.

Even with a consciousness of righteousness and the power of the Godhead, you will still face challenges to the Word of God, and you have to choose to accept His ways over everything else. You want to remember always that maintaining a consciousness of righteousness is intentional and deliberate, it is a choice.

Now we come to the R in A.W.A.R.E. representing Receive.

You woke up, you are walking in Him, and are learning to accept God's way; now you have to fully receive it.

Like the gift of salvation, or in fact, any gift, you can get it, you can have it and own it and still not *receive* it.

I can give you a gift, a present and you can take it and even bring it home with you, but that does not mean that you have actually *received* that gift.

You could have taken the gift home and sat it in a corner and never even opened it. If you never unwrap the gift, did you receive it?

Let us imagine that I gave you a box that I had wrapped up in all the birthday gift bells and whistles. You take that gift home with you, but since you are so distraught over the news that the bank is about to repossess your car, you do not even open the box.

Later, after the tow truck leaves with your car and things settle down, you decide to open the gift. There you find $1,000 in cash. It is a gift not a loan and it would have been more than enough to prevent the bank from taking your car. You had the gift, but since you never received it, you could not use it or actualize it.

Think about that for a minute. You had the gift in your possession. You owned the gift. Yet, you suffered because you did not receive the gift.

You suffered the loss of your car, even though you had the very thing that would have prevented you from losing your car in your possession the whole time. You had it, but you never received it.

Remember our friend in the boat? He had the gift of having everything that he could eat for free; but he never received that gift.

To receive means to take into your heart, fully and completely, and believe it deep down in your heart and soul.

Yes, you already have it, but when you totally *receive* the righteousness of God deep down in your heart and soul, you *activate* your righteousness nature; you turn it on and *release* God's power within you!

To fully activate your righteousness, you need to believe deep in your heart that you are the righteousness of God and confess it with your mouth.

This allows the power of the Holy Spirit to take more control in your life. No, it still does not become automatic, but it becomes a lot easier as it begins to become *second nature,* as it begins to become more natural to you.

It *is* natural to you; it is natural to you now that you have a new nature. But living in your old body and being accustomed to your old mind, you default to your old thoughts.

When you truly take it deep down in your heart, then you rely on what is in you; Christ is in you, and you will not need to learn anything or earn anything; you will just know.

But the anointing which ye have received of him abideth in you, and ye need not that any man teach you: but as the same anointing teacheth you of all things, and is truth, and is no lie, and even as it hath taught you, ye shall abide in him.

---1 John 2:27(KJV)

When you get it deep down, Christ in you can take over.

I've written to warn you about those who are trying to deceive you. But they're no match for what is embedded deeply within you—Christ's anointing, no less! You don't need any of their so-called teaching. Christ's anointing teaches you the truth on everything you need to know about yourself and him, uncontaminated by a single lie. Live deeply in what you were taught.

---1 John 2:27(AMP)

When you believe deep down in your heart and claim it with your mouth that you are the righteousness of God, the Holy Spirit can take charge and that's when you *release* the righteousness within you.

But ye shall receive power, after that the Holy Ghost is come upon you: and ye shall be witnesses unto me both in Jerusalem, and in all Judaea, and in Samaria, and unto the uttermost part of the earth.

---Acts 1:8(KJV)

Yes, just as when you are baptized by the fire of the Holy Spirit, so too will you *release* such power.

You have it, and own it, and walk in it, but now fully receive it. Let me give you an analogy I think will help explain having, yet not receiving, a little better. Let's take a brief look at the history of electricity.

A Brief History of the Use of Electricity

How long have we had electricity? Your first thought might be that we have had electric power for the last few hundred years.

The truth however, is that electricity has been around since the beginning of time. God created electricity during those six days of creation, and remember, He created nothing since then.

In fact, we have had all of the components and everything we needed to make cars, cell phones, flat screen TVs and every so-called luxury that we have today, we had since the beginning of time. But there was a process that we had to go through.

First, electricity terrified people. In the Old Testament no one knew what it was in the sky; the shrieking lights and the horrifying thunder of the electrical storm, caused people to run and hide.

As time went on though, people began to *wake up* to the lightning and thunder and they began to be less afraid of it.

Then around 600 BC, Greek philosophical leaders gained an interest, realizing that there was more to this light than they thought and they began to *walk in it*. They started to check it out and to experiment with it.

Tens of thousands of years passed and still not much more understanding of the scary, heavily born dance that brightened the night skies, but we continued to *walk* in it.

In 1600, English physicist, William Gilbert discovered static electricity and called it, "electricus," as we began to *accept* it.

Then Ben Franklin followed with his key in the kite experiment in 1752, as it still took another 50 years before we began to harness the power of electricity for our use and benefit as we began to *receive* it.

What I want you to see is the pattern there, the path and process it took before we could utilize electricity.

First, we see that God gave us the power. We had the power of electricity from day one...literally. We had the power all the time, but we were asleep to it. We were not aware of it. We were not conscious of it. So first, we had to wake up and become aware of this power.

Then, we began to walk in it; we started to check it out and get involved and started to experiment with it.

Then when we started to accept it; to accept its ways and we began to believe that this strange power could be of beneficial use to us. We also had to accept that it had rules that we had to obey.

Finally, we were able to *receive* it and that is when we came to truly realize and actualize its power. Once we received it, then we were able to *release* it. Are you with me and hear what I say?

Once you come to receive the belief that you are the righteousness of God, deep in your heart, you *release* the power.

Your righteousness will not take over and control you and it is not automatic. However, when you have truly *received* righteousness, you allow the Holy Spirit more control over your life, and He will produce fruit; the fruits of the Spirit.

But the fruit of the Spirit is love, joy, peace, longsuffering, gentleness, goodness, faith,
Meekness, temperance: against such there is no law.

---Galatians 5:22-23(KJV)

When you receive, you activate; you release. To receive is to release.

When you receive the consciousness of righteousness, you release the power.

When you receive the consciousness of righteousness, you release the highest privilege and power to stand firm.

When you receive the consciousness of righteousness, you release the heavenly life.

When you receive the consciousness of righteousness, you release the true strength of your character, your new Christ-like character.

When you receive the consciousness of righteousness, you release the ability to walk in the inheritance of authority, royalty, kingship and queenship.

When you receive the consciousness of righteousness, you release compassion, humility and forgiveness.

When you receive the consciousness of righteousness, you release purity, kindness, obedience and love.

When you receive the consciousness of righteousness, you release the power over sickness and disease.

When you receive the consciousness of righteousness, you release the power over death itself and you begin to embrace the very essence of the meaning of eternity.

Key Consciousness Points – Chapter 8
R = Receive

1. Because you can have a gift, and even own the gift, does not mean that you have actually received the gift.

2. You need to fully *receive* the consciousness of righteousness, even though you know that you have it and are it.

3. There is a process to receive and that comes right after we have woken up, began to walk in it and have accepted God's way.

4. When you fully receive, you actually release.

5. When you fully receive the consciousness of righteousness it releases the full power of the Godhead and you embrace the reality of eternity.

Impartation Prayer

Dear Father,

I truly thank you for the greatest gift ever, the gift of righteousness! I tried hard to earn it, but right now I am aware it is a free gift for all believers including me.

From now on I *receive* it! It is mine and I am your righteousness by the blood of Jesus who washed away all my unrighteousness and exchanged his righteousness nature with my old sin nature to set me free!

Thank you dear Lord! All of my shame, my fears and guilt are gone for the rest of my life. Amen!

CHAPTER 9
E = Eternity

Finally, to fully embrace the whole concept and understanding of the consciousness of righteousness and to truly realize the power contained in the righteousness nature, you will have to come to embrace the meaning of eternity.

Now, this can get a little complex, but bear with me. It is not complicated but it is complex in that our minds, our human minds, usually have a difficult time grasping the things of God.

Most of us see the word and the understanding of eternity only from one point of view; a human point of understanding.

When we think of the word eternity we usually think of *forever*.   When we hear, *"for all eternity…"* we think of, *"For the rest of time."* We think *forever after*. However, eternity means so much more.

We touched on some of the meaning of eternity back in the chapter of the first letter of the anonym of AWARE, the "A" awake. Now, though, we're going to take it to the next level.

Let us start with the Greek meaning as the Hebrew and Greek are quite similar.

Eternity, eternal

Strong's Concordance: 166 - aiónios:

Part of Speech: Adjective

Transliteration: aiónios

Phonetic Spelling: (ahee-o'-nee-os)

Short Definition: eternal, unending

Definition: age-long, and therefore: practically eternal, unending; partaking of the character of that which lasts for an age, as contrasted with that which is brief and fleeting.

So, as we begin again you see the trend to look at the definition of eternity or eternal to mean something that lasts forever or goes on for all time or to the end of time.

As we go deeper we begin to see the word relating to not only time as in the future tense, but *time* itself.

Eternal (**166** /*aiōnios*)

Eternal life operates simultaneously *outside* of time, *inside* of time, and *beyond* time – i.e. what gives time its everlasting meaning for the believer through faith, yet is also time-independent.

Eternal, as in eternal life, operates *outside of time*. It also operates or exists *inside* of time and *beyond* time. It is independent of time. Wow. And...

166 (*aiōnios*) does not focus on the future *per se*, but rather on the *quality* of the *age* (**165** /*aiōn*) it relates to. Thus believers live in "*eternal* (**166** /*aiōnios*) life" right *now*, experiencing this *quality of God's life* now as a *present possession*.

Good God almighty! "...experiencing this *quality of God's life* now as a *present possession.*"

By the way, the short Greek definition of 165 - *aión* is an age, a cycle (of time), especially of the present age as contrasted with the future age, and of one of a series of ages stretching to infinity.

What that says is what I just mentioned, that we look at the word eternal to mean from this present age or time and on into the future; as in *from now on.*

However, what this is saying is that eternal and eternity aligns with God and God's existence. It relates to the qualities of God's life.

So, when the Bible talks about the Christian having eternal life, it is not only talking about something that will happen in the future, but that exists independent of time, and also that shares the quality of life that God has.

Do you see what I say? Eternal life shares quality of life with God! However, let's keep going.

Let's go back to the part that we easily understand; that eternal means never-ending.

Strong's 166 (continued)

3. Without end, never to cease, everlasting

"Joined to thee forever as a sharer of the same eternal life."

Eternal life is to be joined to God, and share the same life! Wow!

"While we look not at the things which are seen, but at the things which are not seen: for the things which are seen are temporal; but the things which are not seen are eternal."
---2 Corinthians 4:18(KJV)

"For perhaps he therefore departed for a season, that thou shouldest receive him for ever;"
---Philemon 15(KJV)

"Perhaps it was for this reason that he was separated from you for a while, so that you would have him back forever,"
---Philemon 15(AMP)

Eternal life is not only about for how long, but to be with Him, joined with Him.

"For so an entrance shall be ministered unto you abundantly
into the everlasting kingdom of our Lord and
Saviour Jesus Christ."

---2 Peter 1:11(KJV)

Okay. So eternal life, eternity, is to be joined with God and share a life with God for a time that does not end, does not cease. Glory to God!

Eternity we know means without end. But wait...

Strong's 166 (continued)

2. Without beginning

"A gospel whose subject-matter is eternal, i.e., the saving purpose of God adopted from eternity."

When we speak of eternity or something that is eternal, it has no ending, but it also has no beginning!

"Now to him that is of power to stablish you according to my
gospel, and the preaching of Jesus Christ, according to the
revelation of the mystery, which was kept secret
since the world began,"

---Romans 16:25(KJV)

*"Who hath saved us, and called us with an holy calling, not
according to our works, but according to his own purpose
and grace, which was given us in Christ Jesus
before the world began,"*

---2 Timothy 1:9(KJV)

Good God! Called to His purpose before the
world began!

*"In hope of eternal life, which God, that cannot lie,
promised before the world began;"*

---Titus 1:2(KJV)

Strong's 166 (continued)

1. Without beginning or end

"That which always has been and always will be."

Eternity is that which has no beginning and no
ending; it simply has always been and will always be.

You might want to let that to sink in and digest
it for a minute. My God.

Thayer's Greek Lexicon – Strong's 166

"Eternity covers the complete philosophic idea — without beginning and without end; also either without beginning or without end; as respects the past, it is applied to what has existed time out of mind.... αἰώνιος (from Plato on) gives prominence to the immeasurableness of eternity (while such words as συνεχής continuous, unintermitted, διατελής perpetual, lasting to the end, are not so applicable to an abstract term, like αἰών); αἰώνιος accordingly is especially adapted to supersensuous things..."

Not paying too much attention to those Greek words as their meanings align with the other words there. But let's break this down for a minute.

"...*also either without beginning or without end; <u>as respects the past</u>, it is applied to what has existed time out of mind...*"

As respects the past... Do you see that? Eternity is applied not only forward, but backward to the past to whatever has existed!

"...gives prominence to the immeasurableness
of eternity..."

The *immeasurableness* of eternity!

You really cannot measure eternity; not in any human sense.

Glory to God! Are you with me? Do you see this? Let me try to calm down and pull this together for you.

Listen, when you are saved, it is an act of eternity. What Jesus did on the cross on Mount Calvary was an act of *eternal redemption*.

"Neither by the blood of goats and calves, but by his own blood he entered in once into the holy place, having obtained eternal redemption for us."

---Hebrews 9:12(KJV)

Jesus, the Christ, obtained eternal redemption for us. That redemption spans all time. Christ redeemed us. But, hold on. Let's look closer at what redemption actually means.

To be *redeemed* does not mean our sins were forgiven or that we were reconciled. No. No.

Redeem by every definition means to buy back, to trade in, to exchange. When you redeem a coupon you trade in the coupon in exchange for the discount.

Merriam Webster

5a: to free from a lien by payment of an amount secured thereby

> b(1): to remove the obligation of by payment, the U.S. Treasury redeems savings bonds on demand
>
> (2): to exchange for something of value.
>
> redeem trading stamps
>
> c: to make good : fulfill

Redeem means to transfer! It means to cash in!
Redeem means to *exchange*!

Jesus, the Lamb of God, cashed Himself in, He exchanged Himself for us!

Jesus exchanged His righteousness for our sinfulness! It was a transfer! And it was an *eternal* redemption and what does eternity mean, again?

Not just for a very long time, not just until the end of the age; not even just until the end of time to forever. No.

Jesus obtained redemption for us for
<u>ALL TIME!</u>
Past, Present and Future!

You are the pure and holy righteousness of Jesus Christ and you have always been, and always will be! In the eyes of God you cannot sin and you have never sinned!

You have always been pure and righteousness since before the world was formed.

You are not a sinner saved by grace. You are not a sinner and you have never ever been a sinner!

"Hold it!" I know someone right now is thinking, "Hold on, there, Joseph. I know some of the things I have done, I am aware of the sins I have committed even after I got saved, and Lord knows some of the things I have done before I got saved. I have asked God to forgive me and I know He has, but I can't forget those things I've done."

Well guess what? That's *your* problem! Seriously. If you need to hold on and remember your sins...you are the only one who does, because God doesn't. God does not even remember your sins.

"For I will be merciful to their unrighteousness, and their sins and their iniquities will I remember no more."

---Hebrews 8:12(KJV)

God does not remember your unrighteousness or your sins or any of your mess and that applies not only to everything that you have done in the past, but the things that you have yet to do. God has blotted those things out of existence.

"I, even I, am he that blotteth out thy transgressions for mine own sake, and will not remember thy sins."

---Isaiah 43:25(KJV)

"Wait a minute, Joseph." You say. "Come on; how can God forget something?"

First of all, it does not say that He forgot. It says that He will remember no more; big difference. But also you have to embrace the idea of eternity. Jesus secured *eternal* redemption for us which means it *always was.*

Some people have a real hard time with this and understanding the idea of eternity. However, you need to embrace the fact that you are the righteousness of God forever and always.

For those who still have a problem with this, here is another way to look at it.

It Wasn't Me

Look back and remember your baptism. Think about your water baptism. If you have not yet been baptized, then I urge you to do so. Remember, water baptism does not ensure or negate your salvation, but God said that it is what we should do. Your baptism in water is a profession of your faith. It is the outward symbolization of the inward change that you received. So, get baptized.

Then remember your baptism and what it meant, what it symbolized. When you were baptized, you died. The old you, your old sinful spirit, died and was buried.

"Therefore we are buried with him by baptism into death: that like as Christ was raised up from the dead by the glory of the Father, even so we also should walk in newness of life."

---Romans 6:4(KJV)

The old you died. So, when the enemy brings up those old things that you have done and accuses you, you can honestly say, "That wasn't me."

It is the truth; that *wasn't* you. It was someone else. Now, when things come up that you have done more recently, like yesterday or this morning, you can still say, "That wasn't me." And you would still be telling the truth.

Eternal Righteousness

As you have now developed the consciousness of righteousness, you must accept and receive that fact that your righteousness is not only forever, it is for all eternity.

You are pure and holy and predestined to share life eternal joined to the almighty God. Your redemption is a product of God and shares His qualities; no beginning and no ending. You did not become righteous when you got saved. You did not become righteous by reading this book and becoming aware of your righteousness. You are the pure and holy righteousness of God.

You always were the pure and holy
righteousness of God.

You will always be pure and holy
righteousness of God!

Key Consciousness Points – Chapter 9
E = Eternity

1. Eternity and things that are eternal are the work of God and exists outside, inside and independent of time.

2. Eternal life means to share life joined to God for all eternity.

3. Eternity means to have no ending; to never cease, but also to have to beginning; to never start.

4. Jesus obtained eternal redemption for us meaning He exchanged His righteousness for our sinfulness for all eternity.

5. You are the pure and holy righteousness of God; you always were and will always be.

Impartation Prayer

Dear Everlasting Father,

How I praise, glorify and magnify Your name for the eternal redemption I received in Jesus, Your holy Son who exchanged His righteousness nature with my old sinful nature for all eternity!

Now I know, I am pure, holy, and righteous and I will always be and have always been!

Thank you! Thank you! And thank you once again! Amen!

CHAPTER 10
Putting it All Together

Amen and God bless you! You have to be feeling much more free right now. You have to be feeling much more powerful right now and more confident and assured of your salvation and of your righteousness nature.

Now I want to just pull it all together for you to help you really, truly embrace all that we went over. I pray that you will take it in and embrace your righteousness as your birthright.

Let's just briefly go over the book and the process to this point, let's do a quick recap.

A Brief Recap

In the first chapter we did an overview of what was to come and laid out the basics of the consciousness of righteousness.

We know that at salvation most of us are so overjoyed at the prospect of having eternal life in Heaven, that we often overlook the other benefits of salvation.

We learned that our righteousness standing actually has absolutely nothing to do with our own personal performance or how holy we are.

We came to understand that all we need to do is become fully aware of our righteousness.

Then we took a look at exactly what the Consciousness of Righteousness is and in doing that, we first examined what it was *not*.

We found that the consciousness of righteousness is not about you or me; it is not about us. It is all about Christ. It is about Christ living in you.

We learned that the meaning of *consciousness* is a *joint-awareness* shared by us and God and that there are two forms of consciousness: the consciousness of sin and the consciousness of righteousness.

Righteousness is the Holy and sin-free purity of the almighty God the Father and we are the righteousness of God through our faith in Christ Jesus.

Then we learned that we need to turn from our consciousness of sin and become aware of our consciousness of righteousness and live in *that* nature.

In the third chapter, we looked at the history of what happened. We saw that Adam and Eve were born in the perfect image of God Himself. They were born pure, holy and the righteousness of God. Adam and Eve sinned and severed their perfect relationship with God, which caused them to live in a state of sin and the consciousness of sin of which we inherited.

However, when Jesus sacrificed and died on the cross, He took our sin and *exchanged* it with His righteous, restoring righteousness to everyone who is born again.

Then we looked at how we can develop our consciousness of righteousness, how we can better unleash the power of God within us.

We realized that while you can fully have a genuine consciousness of righteousness, your body and soul do not automatically or naturally adapt to this new nature and spirit. Therefore, we know that to live in the consciousness of righteousness requires a deliberate and intentional act on our part, an act of faith.

In accomplishing that, a simple plan to remember is A.W.A.R.E. A = Awake, W = Walk, A = Accept, R = Receive, E = Eternal.

In the A = Awake, we found that the first step is for us to wake up and become aware of who we are and what we are. To wake up and accept the fact that our righteousness is not about us and what we do, but about Christ and what He has done.

In the chapter on the W = Walk, we learned that it is time for you and I to begin to walk by faith. We need to begin making decisions based more on our spirit rather than our flesh and what we see.

We also found that faith is persuasion and persuasion is action. Faith requires action. Faith without action, without work, is dead. When we walk by faith, we walk in Him; we walk in the righteousness of God.

As we walk in the fullness of what we are; the righteousness of God, we wield the power of the Godhead over all principalities and power!

In the second A for Accept, we know that we must completely accept God's way in spite of everything else. We have to lean not to our own understanding.

Also, our righteous nature will not take us over and control us; it is not automatic or subconscious. We have to make a deliberate and intentional choice to accept and allow our new nature, our righteous nature to take control.

In Chapter 8, R for Receive, we saw that even though we can get a gift, and even own the gift, it is possible to still not actually have received the gift. We need to fully *receive* the consciousness of righteousness, even though we know that we have it and are it. When we do fully receive it, that releases the power of the Godhead.

Then we took a fascinating look at the E = Eternity. We learned that eternity and things that are eternal are the work of God and exist outside, inside and independent of time.

Eternal life means to share life joined to God for all eternity.

We found that eternity means to have no ending; to never cease, but also to have no beginning; to never start.

Jesus obtained eternal redemption for us, meaning He *exchanged* His righteousness for our sinfulness for all eternity.

We are the pure and holy righteousness of God; we always were and will always be.

Questions

However, I feel I need to address a couple of questions that I know are still on the minds of a few people. I know that lingering in the back of the minds of many of you is one or two nagging questions that can stand as small hurdles that may cause you to stumble on your way to total freedom.

I know that some people are having a hard time with much of the information in this book, in particularly in the last chapter *E = Eternity*.

So to make this easier, I am going to state the questions and the doubt for you. Please allow me to see if I can verbalize the thoughts. I am going to ask myself these questions.

"Okay, Joseph. You say that I am the righteousness of God and that I am now pure and holy. You say that even though I may sin, my spirit cannot sin. You say that Jesus took care of my sin so totally and so completely that He not only removed my past sins, but even sin that I have not even committed yet.

With all of that, Joseph, I have two very good questions for you:

1. If my sins have been forgiven, past, present and future; then when I sin, why do I have to ask God for forgiveness? The Bible clearly says that I need to continually ask for forgiveness. But if I am already forgiven, why do I need to ask?

2. If we have been cleared of all sins, even those we have yet to commit, and if we are saved and righteous, no matter what; in other words, *once saved always saved*, then doesn't that give us a license to sin? People could do whatever they want to do because they know that they will always be saved no matter what. I mean, if people know that there is no punishment for what they do, they will be able to do anything that they please.

Wow! Those are monster questions and I am sure some of you are saying, "Yes! Those are the questions!" They are indeed very good and valid questions too.

Well, I am not psychic, but I know these are critical questions on many people's minds because I am aware of what some people have learned and have grown up to believe. For some, the very idea of *once saved always saved*, is an affront to everything that they believe.

From the information you have received thus far in this book, and the answers I am going to give you here, I pray the Holy Spirit will enlighten you with revelation knowledge of these issues right now, in the name of Jesus! Let's look at these one at a time.

If I am already forgiven, why ask for forgiveness?

First, please understand that when you ask for forgiveness after you commit an act of sin today, is not for God…it is for you.

Remember that sin separates us from God. Our spirits are directly connected to God, but sin separates our minds, our souls and our bodies from Him.

Let me make this clear; God does not push you away. The separation is from **_you_** not God. Your sin creates guilt, shame and fear in you, which pushes *you* away from Him.

When you, or again, the physical parts of you, sin, you cower and begin to hide in the presence of His holiness. This is evident from the beginning of time. Let's go back to Adam and Eve.

"And they heard the voice of the Lord God walking in the garden in the cool of the day: and Adam and his wife hid themselves from the presence of the Lord God amongst the trees of the garden.

And the Lord God called unto Adam, and said unto him, Where art thou?
And he said, I heard thy voice in the garden, and I was afraid, because I was naked; and I hid myself.
---Genesis 3:8-10(KJV)

I could go deep enough into this chapter of Genesis to write a book or two, but I hope this will become obvious to you.

They hid or tried to hide from God. They knew they did wrong and they hid. God did not tell them to go away, in fact He searched for them (of course already knowing exactly where they were and what they did).

This is what happens to us. When we sin, we draw back, we move away from God which puts us in even more danger.

When we sin, we need to draw *closer* to Him. By asking for forgiveness, you simply acknowledge that what you did was wrong, thus freeing your mind and your conscience, and allowing you to move, guilt free into His presence.

Then one might say, "But they were punished. Adam and Eve received harsh punishment for their sin; God kicked them out of the Garden of Eden."

Again, we do not have the time to get too deep into this, but I can tell you that God expelling Adam and Eve from the Garden of Eden was not an act of punishment or retribution; it was an act of grace, mercy and one of the greatest blessings God ever bestowed on humanity.

The point I am making though, is that when you sin, your physical response is to recoil and back away from God, and this is why you need to ask for forgiveness, and know that He will not only forgive you, but He already has, and thus help you remain in close fellowship with Him.

Your act of acknowledging your sin and asking for forgiveness allows your human brain to better reconcile this act of God's love and forgiveness, which is beyond human understanding.

The second reason that you ask for forgiveness, even though you are already forgiven, is that it is simple common courtesy. It is common courtesy to apologize for doing something wrong to someone even if it was a mistake.

You know your spouse will forgive you if you make a particular mistake of doing something that was not quite right, but you still say, "I'm sorry..." don't you?

You know that your husband or wife loves you and will not divorce you just because you forgot to pick up the milk on your way home; but you say, "I'm sorry dear..." anyway.

When you forget their birthday, you know your husband, wife, parent or child is not going to hate you or end your relationship because it slipped your mind. But you say, "I'm sorry. Can you forgive me?" anyway.

So, when you sin against God, whether on purpose or by accident, it only makes sense to say, "I'm sorry, Lord. Please forgive me."

It is simply how you behave and how you treat someone that you love.

Since there is no punishment, then we have a license to sin.

This is a good one and a question that not only do many people have a problem with today, but also many people had with issues back then, during the time when Christ walked the earth.

Unfortunately, this question and understanding the answer, has far too many of our brothers and sisters in Christ trapped and enslaved by a performance-based theology that they live a life of struggle, stress and strife, rather than one of peace, prosperity and power that is their just inheritance.

Let me begin by taking you back to when the Apostle Paul was explaining this to some fellow Christians.

*"For as by one man's disobedience many were made sinners,
so by the obedience of one shall many be made righteous.
Moreover the law entered, that the offence might abound. But
where sin abounded, grace did much more abound:*

That as sin hath reigned unto death, even so might grace reign through righteousness unto eternal life by Jesus Christ our Lord."

---Romans 5:19-21(KJV)

Paul gives a brief overview of what happened as he tells them that by one man's (Adam's) disobedience, many were made sinners.

Also, that by one man's (Jesus') obedience, many were made righteous. Paul continued with...

"Moreover the law entered, that the offence might abound..."

This law, the *Law of Moses*, the commandments, was to edify sin; to make sin abound, by convicting us. This served to help us realize that we were slaves to sin and that we could not save ourselves. The law showed us that we could never behave well enough or perform well enough to make ourselves righteous or work our way into Heaven.

The law was to help us see that we had to have a savior, which paved the way for us to understand that we needed Christ.

"But where sin abounded, grace did much more abound:"

Further, when Christ came, He showed that with all the sin, sin abounding everywhere; that grace always trumped sin. No matter how much sin there was, there was and would always be more grace.

The end result, as Paul explained, is that sin bought with it death, but God's grace brings righteousness unto *eternal* life, through Jesus Christ.

*That as sin hath reigned unto death, even so might grace
reign through righteousness unto eternal life by
Jesus Christ our Lord."*

Good God! Can you see this? Do you hear what I say? Can it be any clearer? But apparently, what Paul said wasn't clear enough, as the next question shows.

*"What shall we say then? Shall we continue in sin,
that grace may abound?"*

---Romans 6:1(KJV)

This is the exact question that many people ask today. "So does this mean we should or could continue to sin and sin, because we have forgiveness? "

The Message Translation puts it this way;

"So what do we do? Keep on sinning so God
can keep on forgiving?"

---Romans 6:1(MSG)

Please note Paul's response.

God forbid. How shall we, that are dead to sin,
live any longer therein?

---Romans 6:2(KJV)

Paul said, "God forbid!"

First, you have to remember that you no longer have a proclivity toward sin. That is, you no longer possess the appetite, tendency or inclination toward sin. Once you are saved, sin no longer has a stranglehold on you and once you come into the full consciousness of your righteousness and confess and believe it in your heart, you then free your mind from sin as well.

Also, let's not forget that we are talking about *individual sins* and not *sin* itself. Remember we talked about this in detail in *Chapter 3: Adam and Eve and The Origin of Sin Consciousness.*

There is sin the verb, as in you committing a sin. However, sin is also a *condition*; it is a *state of being*. To be separated from God is to be in sin. This is how you are born into sin. Through Adam, all sin came into the world. However, Jesus totally and permanently rectified that. Let me give you an analogy.

Look at it like a mango tree. You have this beautiful mango tree that bares delicious mangos. The root of that mango tree is its nature. The root of the mango tree, at first, has a sin nature; the condition of the tree is sin. Therefore, all the fruit for which the tree produces is also sin. Does that make sense?

However, when Jesus remakes the tree, He gives it a new nature; a righteousness nature. Now the very roots of the mango tree bare the condition of righteousness. The result is the fruit the tree it produces is righteous. The mangos have to begin to bare the evidence of their roots. A righteous tree cannot produce unrighteous fruit.

"A good tree cannot bring forth evil fruit, neither can a corrupt tree bring forth good fruit."
---Matthew 7:18(KJV)

Not only are you no longer a slave to or under the control of sin, but you no longer have the appetite or desire to sin. It is really just not in you anymore. Look at it another way.

Let's imagine that the current presidential administration or the ruling body of government, whomever that may be where you live, and at the time you are reading this; declared that there would no longer be any type of punishment to hit old ladies over the head and steal their purses.

Are you with me? Let's assume, for a moment, that suddenly it became perfectly legal to go out and hit an elderly woman over the head, knock her out or even kill her and take her money.

Please think about this question. If that were legal, would you go out and start hitting old ladies over the head and taking their pocketbooks?

Please don't laugh and think that this is a ridiculous question. You may be thinking, "Of course I would never do anything like that!"

Okay, but why not? There is no punishment for it. Nothing will happen; you can still go on with your life. Why would you not commit such an act?

Eventually, you will conclude that such an act is not in you to do. It is not in the roots of who you are. Regardless of if there is punishment or not, you would not do it because it is not something that is in you to do.

Listen; you would not do such a thing because it is not in your *nature* to do! Good God, I'm preaching again!

It does not matter if the punishment was nothing or the death penalty, you would not do it because it is not who you are. Stay with me, I need you to get this.

When you are born again, remember you have a new nature! You have the nature of Christ. You have a righteous nature. You have a nature that does not desire to sin any more.

If beating up little old ladies was not a crime or even if it were not a sin, you still wouldn't do it because it goes against your nature.

God does not need to threaten you to get you to do what is right. If you were born again, your new nature, your new spirit is who you are, and as you grow, you are steadily becoming more like yourself; the real you. As you grow, the fruit on the tree become more of the reflection of your new roots.

Also, God wants you to love Him and to try to be more like Him because you *want* to, not because He threatened you. God is not standing there, holding the threat of burning in hell over your head, if you do not give Him honor. No, no.

In fact, that very scenario, one where you are threatened with life or death if you do not give your undying loyalty to Him, is the operating standard of

The Godfather

not

God *The* Father!

God is not a fat-cheeked, low-talking gangster who demands your loyalty and obedience or else he causes you and maybe your family to disappear.

God is not threatening to send you to hell if you disobey Him or if you mess up. He is also not ready to revoke your ticket to heaven if you make too many mistakes.

To live such an existence is to live in misery; it would be a living hell. If you live in that state now, if you live in constant fear, and under the ever-present threat of losing your passport to heaven; if you are

never sure that you dotted all the I's or crossed every T;
it is time for you to relax and realize that you are free!

You are not kneeling to a mere mortal godfather;
you worship and share eternal life with God *The* Father!

Remember that you are
The pure and holy righteousness of God…

That you always were
The pure and holy righteousness of God…

And that you will always be
The pure and holy righteousness of God

Amen and Amen!

The Consciousness of Righteousness;
You can't learn,
You can't earn it
Just live it!

Contact Joseph Edhuine
or join the conversation at:

www.JosephEdhuineMinistries.org

www.facebook.com/JosephEdhuineMinistries

or email

JosephEdhuine@Gmail.com

13064900R00120

Made in the USA
San Bernardino, CA
20 December 2018